THE EASY
VENISON
COOKBOOK

THE EASY VENISON COOKBOOK

60 SIMPLE RECIPES FOR DEER, ELK, AND MOOSE

BRI VAN SCOTTER

ROCKRIDGE
PRESS

Interior and Cover Designer: Patricia Fabricant
Art Producer: Janice Ackerman
Editor: Pam Kingsley
Production Editor: Andrew Yackira
Cover Photography: © 2020 Hélène Dujardin. Food Styling by Anna Hampton.
Illustration: Courtesy of Creative Market
Author Photo: Courtesy of Leticia Andrade

ISBN: Print 978-1-64739-810-1 | eBook 978-1-64739-485-1
R0

For my sweet daughter, Mila:
Kitchen dances and cooking with you
will always be the best day ever!
Love, Mommy

CONTENTS

INTRODUCTION

I wasn't always a hunter. In fact, for years I was against hunting, yet I had no problem eating steak, a burger, or store-bought chicken. As I grew into my career as a chef, I became increasingly aware of where my food was coming from and how it was raised, and my outrage at the way animals were raised for our nation's food system prompted me to go out and hunt for truly organic protein myself.

Now, as a hunter, I know exactly where my food comes from, I don't take more than I need, and I have so much more appreciation for what I eat. I take part in all aspects of my harvest, from field dressing to the finished dish on the plate, with my hands on that animal throughout the whole process. So, as you can imagine, I make sure to prepare and cook my harvest as perfectly as I can.

While my background as a chef is in fine dining, I readily admit that I don't get to eat like the guests I served every day. When I was starting out in professional kitchens, my meals were often leftovers or random items thrown together in a bowl that I could eat quickly so I could return to my shift.

When I became a mom, I wanted better, and that is how this book came about; its purpose is to show how you can make delicious meals in a short amount of active cooking time and with simple ingredients. It is possible to have a delicious dinner on the table, take care of your family, and not use every pot in your house for one meal. Let appliances like the slow cooker, pressure cooker, and grill, as well as your stovetop and oven, do all the work for you.

I know you're busy, so use this book to help bring a delicious meal to your table in no time.

CHAPTER 1

VENISON BASICS

Consider this chapter Venison 101. Here, we will cover everything you need to know for success in the kitchen, including the factors that affect venison flavor, how to field dress to preserve the quality of your harvest, the different venison cuts and the best cooking methods to use for them, how to work with a venison processor, how to grind your own venison, and more.

TYPES OF VENISON

In the recipes in this book, you will see me calling for venison. Venison refers to the meat of antlered animals, such as white-tailed deer, elk, and moose. Although these animals vary in size, they all have the same cuts, though some will be bigger than others. When following my recipes, use the indicated cut and weight of whatever kind of venison you have.

These animals vary not only in size but also in the flavor of their meat. White-tailed deer have the gamiest flavor, and moose and elk have a smooth and slightly sweet taste. Antelope is very mild in flavor, with notes of sage.

That said, every animal you harvest tastes different because of what it has been feeding on. Other factors that can impact flavor include:

➣→ the age of the animal

➣→ how cleanly you shot the animal

➣→ whether the animal had been running prior to being shot

➣→ how long the animal took to expire

➣→ how fast you were able to field dress and chill the meat

The meat of a young animal tends to be less gamy and more tender, because the animal's muscles haven't been used as much as those of older animals. If you have a perfect shot placement on an animal and it expires almost instantly, your meat will be of higher quality. If the animal took a shot and ran for 500 yards, the meat will be pumped full of adrenaline and not have the same quality. Stress, pain, and adrenaline are huge factors affecting how the meat will taste. If you are not able to chill your harvest quickly, your meat may either have a slight sour note to it when cooked or spoil entirely.

FIELD DRESSING

Field dressing is the very first thing you need to do once your harvest is down and passed. For deer, elk, and moose, field dressing consists of immediately removing the internal organs so you can cool down the internal cavity as rapidly as possible; this helps keep the meat from spoiling. Once you have field dressed your animal, keep the carcass as cool as you can during transport. If you are a long way from a processor or home, place a bag of ice in the cavity to help keep the meat cool. If you are hunting and can't get back to camp easily or quickly, it's best to gut and quarter your harvest. Game bags are especially great to carry when hunting to help keep the meat clean while you are packing out.

VENISON CUTS

Venison cuts are very similar to beef cuts, but they are very different when it comes to tenderness. Deer get much more exercise than domesticated farm cows. Wild deer have to run from predators and find food, so their meat is less tender, drier, and lacks the fat that beef has. However, if you know the cuts and which cooking methods are best for those cuts, you can create venison dishes that are just as tender as beef.

Tender Cuts

Tender cuts are usually the most sought-after pieces of any animal. The most tender and prized muscle on a deer is the backstrap. Due to their lack of tough silver skin and ligaments, tender cuts are great for high cooking temperatures such as grilling or panfrying.

Backstrap and tenderloin: These are the most tender cuts on the animal. They are great for cutting into steaks and grilling or broiling. Since backstrap and tenderloin cuts are both very lean and lack fat, adding oil or butter to the cooking process will give you the best results.

Knuckle: The knuckle is a naturally tender cut from the inside round that's great for roasts, medallions, or even thick steaks. I like to grill and pan sear it or roast it whole.

Ribs and loin: The rib meat and loin are best suited for dry cooking methods such as grilling, broiling, and even panfrying.

Rack: The rack is also known as rib roast. It has the loin still attached to the ribs, and the ribs are usually sawed down to a shorter length than when harvested. A rack makes a stunning presentation and is great roasted whole.

Tough Cuts

The tougher cuts of venison are the highly used muscles of the animal, such as the shoulders and legs. These muscles contain lots of ligaments and silver skin, which makes them best suited for cooking at lower temperatures for long periods of time to break down those tough muscle fibers.

Brisket: Just like beef, there is venison brisket, which comes from the chest area. Venison brisket is much smaller than beef brisket but equally delicious. Treat it the same way, pot roasting or smoking it low and slow; the good news is that it cooks in a fraction of the time, compared to beef brisket.

Round/hindquarter: The hindquarter contains cuts that are great for steak, kebabs, stew meat, jerky, and grinding, including the top round, bottom round, the eye of round, and sirloin.

Rump roast: This comes from exactly where you would think: the rump area of the animal. Rounds can also be found near the rump roast, but a round is more toward the back of the leg (hindquarter). Rump roasts are large and are great for—you guessed it—roasting!

Shank: The shanks come from the legs and are best cooked in a slow cooker, a pressure cooker, or the oven for a long time. The shanks are high in collagen, which turns into gelatin when braised.

Shoulder: The shoulder, top blade, and chuck roasts contain large amounts of ligaments, which makes them better suited to long, slow cooking methods like braising. If you intend to grind this meat, be sure to remove as much of the silver skin as possible beforehand. If you are cooking the shoulder in a smoker or oven, it's fine to leave on some of the silver skin, since it will turn to gelatin during cooking and add moisture to the meat.

Stew meat: If your harvest is broken down by a processor, you'll likely get back a number of packages simply labeled "stew meat." Stew meat often consists of meat taken from the neck, shank, and sometimes the ribs. Stew meat is best cooked low and slow and is great for slow cookers.

GROUND MEAT

When processing your harvest, you or the processor will gather the smaller pieces from different parts of the animal (usually the chuck section, neck, and shanks) to process into ground meat.

Grinding Your Own Meat

Grinding your own is a great way to make use of tougher cuts that might otherwise get tossed. You can use either a meat grinder or a food processor. The most important step in grinding meat properly is to keep everything cold. That includes the equipment you use to grind it, like the grinding plate and other parts of a meat grinder or the bowl, as well as the blade of a food processor, since grinding causes friction, which in turn creates heat. The best way to be sure your meat and equipment are cold enough is to put them in the freezer for at least 30 minutes before using. Cube the meat into 1- to 2-inch pieces, then put it in the freezer for 30 to 45 minutes. This will help the meat stay firm, allowing it to go through the grinder more easily, with less friction.

If using a grinder, I recommend first putting the meat through a coarse plate, then putting it through a fine plate.

If you are using a food processor, fill the bowl only halfway with meat and pulse 8 to 10 times, just 1 second for each pulse, because the food processor creates a lot of friction and can overheat. Never run the food processor continuously.

FOOD SAFETY AND STORAGE

When storing and handling venison, the most important thing is to prevent cross-contamination, which can happen at various stages of food preparation. That's why keeping a clean work surface and clean utensils is very important.

Bacteria thrive in temperatures between 40°F and 140°F, known as the danger zone. Always refrigerate your venison at a temperature below 40°F, or freeze it at a temperature below 0°F. Make sure you have working thermometers in your refrigerator and freezer so you can maintain proper temperatures. When sealed well, venison will keep for up to 5 days in the refrigerator and up to a year in the freezer. For best results, I recommend investing in a vacuum sealer or a chamber vacuum sealer if you can afford it.

THE RECIPES

I've tried to organize the following recipes in a way that will make it easy for you to find what you're looking for, either by type of cut (tender cuts, tougher cuts, ground meat, etc.), the preparation (soups, stews, and chilis, sausage and jerky), or the cooking technique used (grilling, smoking, slow cooker, pressure cooker, etc.).

The prep work for each recipe in this book takes 15 minutes or less to complete, and some of the recipes make tasty use of store-bought convenience foods, though most are made from scratch with fresh ingredients.

You'll also find these handy labels throughout the book, which should further aid you in answering the question *What's for dinner?*

One Pot: Recipes with this label are made entirely in a single pan, keeping cleanup to a minimum.

6-Ingredient: With venison being one of those ingredients, just five additions make dinner. Salt, pepper, and oil are not included in the ingredient count.

30-Minute: With these recipes, you can have dinner on the table in 30 minutes or less, including prep and cook times.

Pressure Cooker: These recipes are either made in an electric pressure cooker or include a variation for making them in a pressure cooker.

Slow Cooker: These recipes are either made in a slow cooker or include a variation for making them in a slow cooker.

WHAT YOU NEED TO KNOW ABOUT CWD

Chronic Wasting Disease (CWD) is a contagious neurological disease that affects antlered animals like deer, elk, sika deer, moose, and reindeer. Infected animals experience brain degeneration that results in emaciation, abnormal behavior, and eventually death. If you suspect your harvest had CWD, it is recommended that you do not eat it, that you report it your state wildlife department, and that you properly dispose of the carcass as to not infect more wildlife.

If you harvest an animal in an area where animals with CWD have been reported, err on the side of caution when processing meat—to avoid contamination, do not cut through the spinal cord or brain, and debone all the meat.

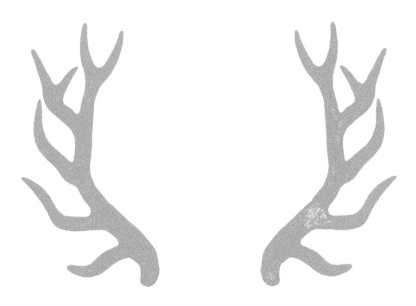

CHAPTER 2

THE TENDER CUTS

Tender cuts are decadent and satisfying and often quick-cooking, making them great for easy meal planning. But be careful not to overcook them, because that can drastically alter their texture. Use an instant-read thermometer, and pull the meat off the heat as soon as it reaches your desired internal temperature.

TENDERLOIN SALAD WITH POMEGRANATE VINAIGRETTE

Who knew venison could be so tasty in salads? This is one of my favorite venison salads, but play around with it—add some pears, grapes, or chopped fresh herbs like chives or tarragon if you're feeling fancy.

Prep Time: 15 minutes
Cook Time: 10 minutes
Serves: 4

3 tablespoons
   pomegranate juice

2 tablespoons red wine vinegar

1 tablespoon Dijon mustard

1 tablespoon honey

Kosher salt

Freshly ground black pepper

⅔ cup extra-virgin olive oil

1 (1-pound) venison tenderloin

2 tablespoons vegetable oil

5 ounces mixed greens

⅓ cup crumbled goat cheese

¼ cup dried cranberries

¼ cup walnut halves, toasted
   and chopped

1. Preheat the broiler with the top rack positioned 5 to 6 inches away from the heat source.

2. In a medium bowl, whisk together the pomegranate juice, vinegar, mustard, honey, and salt and pepper to taste. Drizzle in the olive oil while whisking until well blended.

3. Place a large cast-iron skillet in the oven until hot, about 2 minutes. Season the tenderloin on all sides with the salt and pepper. Remove the pan and add the vegetable oil, tilting the pan to coat the bottom with oil. Add the tenderloin to the pan and place it on the rack near the broiler. Cook for 2 to 3 minutes per side or until the internal temperature reaches 130°F (for rare), or continue cooking for your desired degree of doneness. Transfer to a cutting board.

4. In a large bowl, toss 3 tablespoons of the vinaigrette (or to taste) with the mixed greens, and divide the salad among 4 plates. Top each serving with the goat cheese, cranberries, and walnuts. Thinly slice the venison, arrange it on top, and serve immediately.

Pro Tip: This recipe makes more vinaigrette than needed, because I love having it handy in the refrigerator, where it will keep for up to a week. I also like to use it as a marinade or reduce it in a pan to make a sauce.

KIMCHI-MARINATED TENDERLOIN IN LETTUCE CUPS

I love kimchi! I love to use it as a marinade because it imparts an umami flavor that is hard to achieve with other ingredients. Kimchi has become very popular and can be found in most large supermarkets.

Prep Time: 10 minutes, plus 24 hours to marinate
Cook Time: 20 minutes
Serves: 4 to 6

½ cup plus 2 teaspoons soy sauce, divided

1 cup apple juice

1 cup kimchi

½ medium onion, cut into several pieces

5 garlic cloves, peeled

1 teaspoon sesame oil

1 teaspoon freshly ground black pepper, plus more to taste

2 pounds venison tenderloin

Kosher salt

2 tablespoons vegetable oil

¼ cup chopped scallions

¼ cup grapeseed oil or vegetable oil

1 tablespoon minced or grated fresh ginger

1 tablespoon sherry vinegar

1 head Bibb lettuce, separated into leaves

1. Preheat the oven to 450°F.

2. In a blender, combine ½ cup of the soy sauce, the apple juice, kimchi, onion, garlic, sesame oil, and pepper. Process until well blended and slightly smooth in consistency.

3. Place the venison in a zip-top plastic bag, pour in the marinade, seal, and refrigerate for 24 hours.

4. Heat a large cast-iron skillet over medium-high heat. Remove the tenderloins from the marinade, discarding the marinade, and season with salt and pepper to taste. Add the 2 tablespoons vegetable oil to the skillet. Sear the tenderloins for about 3 minutes per side. Transfer the skillet to the oven to finish cooking for 7 to 10 minutes or until the internal temperature reaches 140°F (for medium) or the meat reaches your desired degree of doneness.

5. Transfer the venison to a cutting board, cover it loosely with foil, and let it rest for 5 minutes.

6. While the meat rests, in a small bowl, stir together the scallions, grapeseed oil, ginger, vinegar, and remaining 2 teaspoons soy sauce.

7. To serve, slice the venison ¼ to ½ inch thick. Arrange the slices on a serving plate, and serve the sauce in a small bowl with a spoon. Have diners place 3 or 4 slices in each lettuce cup, top with the scallion-ginger sauce, and enjoy.

Pro Tip: Venison tenderloin size can vary, and they are often cut in half during processing. That's why I call for 2 pounds of tenderloin instead of a single tenderloin.

HERB-CRUSTED RACK OF VENISON WITH ROASTED BABY POTATOES

If you want to make a dish that's a showstopper, this is it. It's the perfect meal for a holiday gathering, celebration, or those days when you just want to feel like a badass chef—and no one will guess just how easy it was to prepare. This recipe is all about the venison and fresh herbs. If you really want to go all out, smoke this rack on the grill.

Prep Time: 20 minutes
Cook Time: 35 minutes
Serves: 6

1 (2½- to 3-pound) rack of venison, frenched if you like (see Pro Tip)

Kosher salt

Freshly ground black pepper

¼ cup grapeseed oil or vegetable oil

8 garlic cloves, peeled

¾ cup panko bread crumbs

1 small bunch fresh parsley, large stems removed

¼ cup coarsely chopped fresh chives

1 tablespoon coarsely chopped fresh rosemary

¾ cup grated Parmesan cheese, divided

2 tablespoons whole-grain Dijon mustard

2 pounds baby potatoes, quartered (if medium) or halved (if small)

3 tablespoons olive oil

1. Preheat the oven to 400°F

2. Season the venison on both sides with salt and pepper to taste.

3. Heat the grapeseed or vegetable oil in a large cast-iron skillet over high heat until hot. Sear the venison for 3 to 4 minutes per side. Transfer the rack to a large rimmed baking sheet.

4. In a food processor, combine the garlic, panko bread crumbs, parsley, chives, rosemary, and ½ cup of the Parmesan. Pulse until the mixture is well combined and finely chopped.

5. Brush all the sides of the venison rack with the mustard. Press the panko mixture all over the meat to create a thick crust.

6. Scatter the potatoes on the baking sheet. Drizzle with the olive oil and season with salt and pepper to taste. Use your hands to coat the potatoes with the oil. Position the venison in the center of the potatoes. Roast for 25 minutes or until the internal temperature in the center of the rack reaches 130°F (for rare), or the meat reaches your desired

degree of doneness, and the potatoes are tender.

7. Transfer the rack to a cutting board, and let it rest for 5 to 8 minutes before cutting into chops. Toss the potatoes with the remaining ¼ cup Parmesan and serve.

Pro Tip: For an elegant presentation, you can french the rack before roasting it. Using a paring knife, carve away the meat and connective tissue between the first few inches of the long bones.

PAN-SEARED BACKSTRAP STEAKS WITH BEER CHEESE

6-INGREDIENT | 30-MINUTE

Beer cheese and venison is the combo you never knew you were looking for. If you'd like the cheese to have a bit of zip, feel free to add chili powder, minced jalapeños, or your choice of hot sauce (sriracha works nicely) to taste along with the mustard. Serve this with a baked potato or steamed vegetables.

Prep Time: 10 minutes
Cook Time: 20 minutes
Serves: 4

1 cup beer

2 cups shredded sharp cheddar cheese

1 (8-ounce) package cream cheese

1 teaspoon kosher salt, plus more for seasoning

1 teaspoon Dijon mustard

5 tablespoons unsalted butter

4 (6- to 8-ounce) venison backstrap steaks, cut 1 inch thick

Freshly ground black pepper

1. In a medium saucepan, bring the beer to a boil over medium-high heat. As soon as it boils, remove it from the heat. Add the cheddar, cream cheese, 1 teaspoon salt, and mustard and stir with a wooden spoon until melted, smooth, and combined. Cover with a lid and let sit over very low heat while you sear the steaks.

2. In a large cast-iron skillet, melt the butter over medium-high heat. Pat the steaks dry with a paper towel and season with salt and pepper on both sides. Add the steaks to the skillet and cook for 3 to 4 minutes per side or until the internal temperature reaches 130°F (for rare), or the meat reaches your desired degree of doneness.

3. Transfer the steaks to a platter and let rest for about 3 minutes. To serve, drizzle the beer cheese over the venison steaks.

Pro Tip: Once you master this easy beer cheese recipe, start adding other flavorful ingredients, like shallots, garlic, or cayenne, to change things up a bit.

SKILLET-ROASTED BACKSTRAP WITH BERRY-MINT SAUCE

I believe that what an animal eats will pair well on the table. Meaning, if a deer is feasting on berries, berries are going to pair beautifully with venison. I first made this sauce on a hunt in Texas, and it was a slam dunk. It's a great recipe to keep in your pocket for just about all wild game, including waterfowl.

Prep Time: 10 minutes
Cook Time: 25 minutes
Serves: 4

For the berry-mint sauce
1 (16-ounce) bag frozen mixed berries

Juice of 1 orange

3 tablespoons unsalted butter

2 tablespoons chopped fresh mint

1 tablespoon balsamic vinegar

1 bay leaf

1 sprig fresh rosemary

For the backstrap
3 tablespoons unsalted butter

1 tablespoon olive oil

1 (2-pound) venison backstrap, cut in half

Kosher salt

Freshly ground black pepper

1. Preheat the oven to 375°F.

2. **To make the berry-mint sauce:** In a medium saucepan, combine the frozen berries, orange juice, butter, mint, vinegar, bay leaf, and rosemary. Bring to a simmer over low heat, and simmer for 10 minutes.

3. **To prepare the backstrap:** In a large cast-iron pan over high heat, melt the butter with the oil. Season the backstrap with salt and pepper to taste. Add the backstrap to the hot pan, and sear for about 3 minutes per side. Transfer the skillet to the oven and roast for 15 minutes or until the internal temperature of the meat reaches 135°F for medium-rare, or the meat reaches your desired degree of doneness.

4. Transfer the backstrap to a cutting board, let it rest for 5 minutes, then cut the meat into 1-inch slices. Serve the meat topped with the berry-mint sauce, removing the bay leaf before serving.

Pro Tip: You can vacuum seal the cooled sauce in a plastic bag and keep it in the freezer for up to 3 months.

VENISON STEAKS WITH COLCANNON POTATOES

This is a refined version of steak and potatoes, and it's also a clever way to get everyone to eat more vegetables. It's easy and oh so delicious.

Prep Time: 10 minutes
Cook Time: 20 minutes
Serves: 4

For the colcannon potatoes
3 large russet potatoes, peeled and diced

¼ cup sour cream

3 tablespoons unsalted butter

2 teaspoons kosher salt

1 cup frozen chopped spinach, thawed

Freshly ground black pepper

For the venison steaks
4 venison medallions cut from backstrap, 4 to 5 inches wide and about ½ inch thick

1 tablespoon kosher salt

2 teaspoons freshly ground black pepper

2 teaspoons garlic powder

3 tablespoons olive oil

1. **To make the colcannon potatoes:** Bring a large pot of water to boil, then add the potatoes. Cook until the potatoes are tender, about 10 minutes. Drain the potatoes, return the pot to low heat, and add the sour cream, butter, salt, and spinach. Mash together, then season with pepper to taste and adjust the salt if needed. Remove the pot from the heat, and cover it to keep the potatoes warm while the steaks cook.

2. **To prepare the venison steaks:** Pat the venison medallions dry with a paper towel. In a small bowl, combine the salt, pepper, and garlic powder. Season the medallions on both sides with the seasoning mixture.

3. Heat the oil a large cast-iron skillet over medium-high until hot. Add the medallions and cook for 1 to 2 minutes on each side or until the internal temperature reaches 130°F for rare, or until the meat reaches your desired degree of doneness.

4. Transfer the medallions to a cutting board; let them rest for 1 minute before serving over the potatoes.

HOME ON THE RANGE CASSEROLE

Tater tots are probably my favorite frozen food item. I can always find ways to use them for breakfast, lunch, or dinner. This recipe is totally a mom hack— it's easy to make, it's filling, and my family loves it. Plus, it makes amazing leftovers and freezes well; follow the recipe through step 3, then freeze. Thaw it in the refrigerator overnight and increase the bake time to 1 hour and 15 minutes.

Prep Time: 15 minutes
Cook Time: 50 minutes
Serves: 8

1 pound venison backstrap, cut into ½-inch dice

1 (10.5-ounce) can cream of mushroom soup

1½ cups frozen corn kernels

2 cups shredded cheddar cheese, divided

1 small onion, diced

½ cup sour cream

½ cup whole milk

8 strips bacon, cooked until crisp and crumbled

½ teaspoon kosher salt

½ teaspoon freshly ground black pepper

1 (32-ounce) bag frozen tater tots

1. Preheat the oven to 375°F

2. In a 9-by-13-inch baking pan, combine the venison, mushroom soup, corn, 1½ cups of the cheese, the onion, sour cream, milk, bacon, salt, and pepper until thoroughly mixed. Arrange the tots on top in an even layer without any space in between.

3. Bake for 40 to 50 minutes, until hot and bubbling. Sprinkle the remaining ½ cup cheese over the top, then return the pan to the oven and bake until the cheese is melted, about 5 minutes.

Slow Cooker Variation: Follow step 2, combining the ingredients in a 5- to 6-quart slow cooker. Arrange the tater tots on top. Cover and cook for 5 hours on Low. Sprinkle with the remaining cheese, cover, and cook for 30 more minutes.

VENISON ADOBO

30-MINUTE | SLOW COOKER | PRESSURE COOKER

My travels play a huge role in my recipe development, and this is a classic case. During my time diving in the Philippines, when I wasn't eating mangos I was busy eating adobo. I fell head over heels in love with adobo, a simple dish that is packed with flavor. I like to serve mine over rice, and if I'm feeling feisty, I add some steamed vegetables.

Prep Time: 5 minutes
Cook Time: 15 minutes on High Pressure, plus 10 minutes natural release
Serves: 4 to 6

2 pounds venison rump roast, cut into 1-inch cubes

1 large yellow onion, chopped

2 tablespoons minced garlic

4 bay leaves

⅔ cup soy sauce

½ cup apple cider vinegar

½ cup canned full-fat coconut milk

1. Place the venison, onion, garlic, bay leaves, soy sauce, vinegar, and coconut milk in a 6- to 8-quart electric pressure cooker. Stir together to combine.

2. Lock the lid and close the steam valve. Select Manual and set the time for 15 minutes on High Pressure.

3. When the timer sounds, turn it off and let the pressure release naturally for 10 minutes, then quick release any remaining pressure. Remove the bay leaf before serving.

Slow Cooker Variation: Combine all the ingredients in a slow cooker, cover, and cook on High for 5 hours or on Low for 8 to 10 hours.

Short-Cut Tip: Store-bought adobo marinade (I like the Mama Sitas brand) can be substituted for the soy sauce, vinegar, and coconut milk.

VENISON RAGÙ

If there was ragù on the menu when I was in Italy, I was ordering it! Traditionally, it is simmered low and slow for hours to bring out the flavors, and the slow cooker does that perfectly. But don't worry if you're rushed for time; you can also achieve delicious results in a pressure cooker. Double this recipe and keep some in the freezer—ragù gets better with time.

Prep Time: 15 minutes
Cook Time: 6 hours on High or 8 to 10 hours on Low
Serves: 6 to 8

1 (28-ounce) can crushed tomatoes

¼ cup tomato paste

1 large onion, diced

2 medium carrots, diced

2 celery stalks, diced

2 cups beef broth

1 cup dry red wine

2 tablespoons minced garlic

1 teaspoon dried thyme

1 (2-pound) venison knuckle, cut into 2-inch pieces

1 tablespoon kosher salt

2 teaspoons freshly ground black pepper

4 bay leaves

16 ounces pappardelle pasta

Grated Parmesan cheese

1. Place the crushed tomatoes, tomato paste, onion, carrots, celery, broth, wine, garlic, and thyme in a 5- to 6-quart slow cooker. Stir together until well combined. Season the venison with the salt and pepper, then add it and the bay leaves to the slow cooker, pushing the meat down into the mixture.

2. Cover and cook on High for 6 hours or on Low for 8 to 10 hours.

3. Remove the bay leaves from the ragù, then use two forks to shred the venison into pieces in the slow cooker.

4. About 10 minutes before the sauce is finished, prepare the pasta according to the package directions.

5. Serve the ragù on top of the pappardelle, sprinkled with Parmesan.

Pressure Cooker Variation: Follow step 1, combining the ingredients in an electric pressure cooker. Lock the lid and close the steam valve. Select Manual and set the time to 30 minutes on High Pressure. Quick release the steam.

EASY VENISON TIKKA MASALA

SLOW COOKER | PRESSURE COOKER

We all have that dish that we run to when we need a little extra comfort in our life. Tikka masala is that dish for me. Typically, this recipe takes a while to prepare, so I also created a shortcut pressure-cooker variation if you don't have the time. It's delicious served over steamed basmati rice.

Prep Time: 5 minutes
Cook Time: 4 hours on High or 6 to 8 hours on Low
Serves: 4 to 6

2 cups tomato sauce

¾ cup whole-milk Greek yogurt

3 tablespoons curry powder

2 tablespoons lemon juice

1 large onion, diced

2 tablespoons minced garlic

2 pounds venison knuckle, cut into 1-inch cubes

1. Place the tomato sauce, yogurt, curry powder, lemon juice, onion, and garlic in a 5- to 6-quart slow cooker; whisk to combine. Stir in the venison.

2. Cover and cook on High for 5 hours or on Low for 8 to 10 hours.

Pressure Cooker Variation: Follow step 1, combining all the ingredients except the lemon juice in an electric pressure cooker. Lock the lid and close the steam valve. Select Manual and set the time for 10 minutes on High Pressure. Quick release the steam, then stir in the lemon juice.

CHAPTER 3

THE TOUGHER CUTS

If you take away one thing from this chapter on tougher cuts, remember this: low and slow. Tougher cuts need lower temperatures and slower (longer) cook times than tender cuts do. This combination of time and temperature helps to break down all the tendons, cartilage, and intermuscular fats, which results in tender meat with lots of flavor. As you'll see in the recipes that follow, the slow cooker is my tool of choice for preparing tougher cuts of meats. However, thanks to electric pressure cookers, some of these recipes can also be made quickly because pressure cooking mimics low-and-slow cooking for great flavor in a fraction of the time.

WOK-SEARED VENISON WITH GREEN BEANS

30-MINUTE | ONE POT

This is my venison version of one of my favorite Chinese takeout dishes. It's a perfect weeknight dinner, especially when you serve it over rice. The key to this dish is making sure you cut the flank steak against the grain for the most tender meat.

Prep Time: 15 minutes
Cook Time: 15 minutes
Serves: 4

1 cup beef broth

¼ cup oyster sauce

3 tablespoons soy sauce

3 tablespoons rice wine vinegar

1 teaspoon red pepper flakes

3 tablespoons vegetable
   oil, divided

1 pound green beans, trimmed
   and cut in half

1 pound venison flank steak,
   sliced against the grain into
   1-inch pieces

8 scallions, cut into
   1-inch pieces

4 garlic cloves, minced

1 tablespoon minced or grated
   fresh ginger

1. In a small bowl, whisk together the broth, oyster sauce, soy sauce, vinegar, and red pepper flakes.

2. Heat 1 tablespoon of the oil in a wok or large cast-iron skillet over high heat. When the oil is hot, add the green beans and cook, stirring for 4 to 5 minutes or until the beans are bright green and crisp-tender. Transfer to a plate.

3. Add 1 tablespoon of the oil to the wok, then add the venison and cook, stirring occasionally, until browned, 4 to 5 minutes. Transfer the venison to the plate with the green beans.

4. Add the remaining tablespoon of oil to the wok. Add the scallions and cook, stirring, until browned, about 2 minutes. Add the garlic and ginger and cook, stirring, for 30 seconds.

5. Return the green beans and venison to the wok. Add the broth mixture and cook, stirring continuously, for 2 minutes or until the sauce has thickened. Serve immediately.

PHILLY CHEESESTEAK SLIDERS

SLOW COOKER | PRESSURE COOKER

Nothing beats a warm and cheesy Philly cheesesteak sandwich, am I right? I like to cook the roast for this recipe in the slow cooker, which makes the meat super tender and flavorful and easy to shred. I prefer to top my steak with Cheez Whiz, but since it may not be everyone's thing, I have replaced it here with the much-debated alternative, provolone. Why not try it both ways?

Prep Time: 10 minutes
Cook Time: 5 hours on High or 8 to 10 hours on Low
Serves: 4

1 (2-pound) venison roast

Kosher salt

Freshly ground black pepper

2 green bell peppers, halved, seeded, and sliced

2 red bell peppers, halved, seeded, and sliced

1 large onion, thinly sliced

2 tablespoons minced garlic

1 (14.5-ounce) can beef broth

4 soft hoagie rolls

8 slices provolone cheese (or 1 jar Cheez Whiz)

1. Season the venison roast generously with salt and pepper on all sides, then place it in a 6- to 8-quart slow cooker. Add the bell peppers, onion, garlic, and broth.

2. Cover and cook on High for 5 hours or on Low for 8 to 10 hours.

3. Use two forks to shred the meat right in the slow cooker, then mix well with the sauce.

4. To serve, place 1 cup of the shredded meat mixture inside each hoagie roll, top with provolone or Cheez Whiz, and serve immediately.

Pressure Cooker Variation: In step 1, combine the ingredients in an electric pressure cooker. Lock the lid and close the steam valve. Select Manual and set the time for 60 minutes on High Pressure. Naturally release the steam for 15 to 20 minutes, then quick release any remaining steam.

VENISON TACOS AL PASTOR

SLOW COOKER | PRESSURE COOKER

The best tacos I have ever had were from a tiny gas station in Pescadero, California. They were simple yet complex and captivating. This recipe is inspired by those tacos, and tastes so fresh and flavorful with the combination of pineapple and spicy sauce. Feel free to halve the ingredients if you're serving a smaller crowd.

Prep Time: 15 minutes
Cook Time: 6 hours on High or 8 to 10 hours on Low
Serves: 12

1 (16-ounce) jar red
　enchilada sauce

½ cup pineapple juice

¼ cup lime juice

3 tablespoons packed
　brown sugar

3 tablespoons taco seasoning

1 medium onion,
　coarsely chopped

4 garlic cloves, peeled

3 to 4 pounds venison
　stew meat

24 corn tortillas, warmed

1 cup finely shredded
　red cabbage

1 cup diced pineapple

3 tablespoons chopped fresh
　cilantro

Lime wedges, for serving

1. Place the enchilada sauce, pineapple juice, lime juice, brown sugar, taco seasoning, onion, and garlic cloves in a 6- to 8-quart slow cooker and stir to combine. Add the venison and press the pieces into the sauce mixture.

2. Cover and cook on High for 6 hours or on Low for 8 to 10 hours, until the meat is very tender.

3. Using two forks, shred the meat right in the slow cooker, then mix well with the sauce.

4. To assemble, fill each warm tortilla with ¼ cup of meat, making sure to let as much sauce as possible drip from the meat before you place it on the tortilla. Top with cabbage, pineapple, cilantro, and a squeeze of lime. Enjoy.

Pressure Cooker Variation: In step 1, combine the ingredients in an electric pressure cooker. Lock the lid and close the steam valve. Select Manual and set the time for 30 minutes on High Pressure. Quick release the steam. Pick up with step 3.

VENISON SHOULDER CHIPOTLE TACOS

SLOW COOKER | PRESSURE COOKER

Look no further: Your new favorite taco recipe is right here, ready to make your Tuesdays more exciting. Venison and chipotles go together like peas and carrots in my book. The smokiness of the chiles pair beautifully with the sweet gamy flavor of venison. And, best of all, these tacos are super easy to make—just put the ingredients in the slow cooker, and the work is done.

Prep Time: 10 minutes
**Cook Time: 5 hours on High or
8 to 10 hours on Low**
Serves: 8

3 pounds boneless venison chuck, trimmed and cut into 2-inch pieces

¼ cup chopped canned chipotles in adobo sauce

¼ cup lime juice

1 large onion, diced

1 tablespoon chopped garlic

2 bay leaves

16 corn tortillas, warmed

2 cups finely shredded cabbage

½ cup crumbled cotija cheese

1. Place the venison, chipotles, lime juice, onion, garlic, and bay leaves in a 6- to 8-quart slow cooker and mix well.

2. Cover and cook on High for 5 hours or on Low for 8 to 10 hours.

3. Use two forks to shred the meat right in the slow cooker, then mix well with the sauce.

4. To assemble, fill each warm tortilla with ¼ cup of meat. Top with some cabbage and cheese. Remove the bay leaves before serving.

Pressure Cooker Variation: Follow step 1, combining all the ingredients in an electric pressure cooker. Lock the lid and close the steam valve. Select Manual and set the time for 30 minutes on High Pressure. Quick release the steam. Pick up with step 3.

VENISON STROGANOFF

You know that boxed Stroganoff your mom made as a kid that you loved so much? Well, this one is better! Not only is it fresher and tastier, but this home-made version is also just as quick and easy to fix as your favorite boxed one was. It's my go-to pressure cooker recipe, and I always keep the ingredients on hand for last-minute meals. The leftovers are excellent, too.

Prep Time: 10 minutes
Cook Time: 25 minutes
Serves: 6

2 pounds venison stew meat

Kosher salt

Freshly ground black pepper

8 ounces cremini mushrooms, sliced

1 large onion, diced

2 (10.75-ounce) cans condensed cream of mushroom soup

3 cups beef broth

1 cup half-and-half

1½ teaspoons garlic powder

2 teaspoons Worcestershire sauce

16 ounces egg noodles

1 cup sour cream

1. Season the venison stew meat generously with salt and pepper, then place it in a 6- to 8-quart electric pressure cooker. Add the mushrooms, onion, soup, broth, half-and-half, garlic powder, and Worcestershire sauce. Stir to combine.

2. Lock the lid and close the steam valve. Select Manual and set the time for 15 minutes on High Pressure.

3. When the timer sounds, quick release the steam. Open the lid and stir in the egg noodles. Lock the lid, select Manual, and set the time for 5 minutes on High Pressure.

4. When the timer goes off, quick release the steam. Stir in the sour cream and serve immediately.

CARIBBEAN-STYLE VENISON SHOULDER

SLOW COOKER | PRESSURE COOKER

If there is one thing I learned while traveling throughout the Caribbean, it's how magical the combination of sweet fruit like pineapple and warming spices can be. Something special happens when those ingredients come together to highlight the delicious flavor of venison. I serve this dish family style with white rice and black beans.

Prep Time: 5 minutes
Cook Time: 60 minutes on High Pressure, plus 20 minutes natural release
Serves: 12

3 cups pineapple juice

1 cup lime juice

1 large onion, diced

2 tablespoons chopped garlic

1 teaspoon ground allspice

¼ teaspoon cayenne pepper

1 (3- to 4-pound) bone-in venison shoulder roast

Kosher salt

Freshly ground pepper

1. Combine the pineapple juice, lime juice, onion, garlic, allspice, and cayenne in a 6- to 8-quart electric pressure cooker. Stir to combine.

2. Season the venison roast generously with salt and pepper on all sides, then place it in the cooker.

3. Lock the lid and close the steam valve. Select Manual and set the time for 60 minutes on High Pressure. Naturally release the steam for 15 to 20 minutes. Quick release any remaining steam.

4. Shred the meat off the bone using two forks. Discard the bones, and mix the shredded meat with the sauce. Serve immediately.

Slow Cooker Variation: Follow steps 1 and 2 using a slow cooker. Cover and cook on High for 5 hours or on Low for 8 to 10 hours. Pick up with step 4.

GUINNESS-BRAISED VENISON SHORT RIBS

ONE POT | PRESSURE COOKER

Venison ribs are usually scrapped for ground meat, but they are probably my favorite cut on the deer. Be sure to ask your processor to save the ribs for you; otherwise, you'll miss out on delicious recipes like this one.

Prep Time: 15 minutes
Cook Time: 2 hours
Serves: 4

4 pounds bone-in venison short ribs

Kosher salt

Freshly ground black pepper

3 tablespoons olive oil

2 (12-ounce) bottles Guinness Extra Stout

1 (32-ounce) container beef broth

2 cups brewed coffee

2 large onions, diced

1½ teaspoons dried thyme

1 pound baby red potatoes (optional)

1. Preheat the oven to 325°F.

2. Score the short ribs by making a small cut on the back side of the silver skin in between each rib on the meat; cut just enough to slice the silver skin and not the meat. Then, cut the rack into 3- to 4-rib sections. Season the short ribs generously with salt and pepper.

3. Heat the olive oil in an 8-quart Dutch oven over medium-high heat until hot. Working in batches, sear the short ribs for about 2 minutes per side, until browned. Transfer to a plate and continue with the remaining ribs.

4. Reduce the heat to low. Add the Guinness, broth, coffee, onions, thyme, and potatoes (if using), then return the ribs and any accumulated juices to the pot.

5. Cover the pot and transfer it to the oven. Braise until the meat is falling-off-the-bone tender, about 2 hours.

Pressure Cooker Variation: Prep the venison short ribs as directed in step 2. Select Sauté and sear them in the oil as directed in step 3. Add the other ingredients, lock the lid, and close the steam valve. Select Manual and set the time for 45 minutes on High Pressure. Naturally release the steam for 15 minutes; quick release any remaining steam.

VENISON OSSO BUCCO

SLOW COOKER | PRESSURE COOKER

Shanks are often a forgotten cut, but, in my opinion, they are one of the most delicious parts of the animal. The key to cooking this dish is to remove the sinew and silver skin and cook the meat at a lower temperature for a longer period of time to turn a normally tough cut into fork-tender goodness. Serve the shanks with mashed potatoes or creamy polenta.

Prep Time: 15 minutes
Cook Time: 5 hours on High or 8 to 10 hours on Low
Serves: 4

4 venison bone-in shanks, cut crosswise into 2-inch-thick pieces

Kosher salt

Freshly ground pepper

¼ cup all-purpose flour

3 tablespoons olive oil

1 large onion, diced

1 medium carrot, diced

1 large celery stalk, diced

1 tablespoon chopped garlic

2 sprigs fresh thyme

1 cup red wine

1 cup beef broth

1 (14.5-ounce) can crushed tomatoes

1. Gently pat the venison shanks dry with a paper towel, then season them generously with salt and pepper. Dredge the shanks in the flour so they have a thin coating all around.

2. Heat the oil in a large cast-iron skillet over high heat. When the oil is hot, add 2 of the shanks and sear until they are browned all over, about 2 minutes per side. Transfer to a plate and repeat with the remaining shanks.

3. Transfer the shanks and any accumulated juices to a 6- to 8-quart slow cooker. Add the onion, carrot, celery, garlic, thyme, wine, broth, and tomatoes.

4. Cover and cook on High for 5 hours or on Low for 8 to 10 hours.

Pressure Cooker Variation: In step 2, combine the ingredients in an electric pressure cooker. Lock the lid and close the steam valve. Select Manual and set the time for 45 minutes on High Pressure. Naturally release the steam for 15 to 20 minutes, then quick release the remaining steam.

CUBAN-STYLE VENISON ROAST

SLOW COOKER | PRESSURE COOKER

Oh, heavens, this is delicious! It's not only good on its own, but it also makes the best Cuban sandwich you will ever have. Serve this as a main dish or as a sandwich—you really can't go wrong. All the citrus in this recipe makes the venison beyond tender. I like to serve it with mango rice and black beans.

Prep Time: 15 minutes
Cook Time: 5 hours on High or 8 to 10 hours on Low
Serves: 4 to 6

1 large onion, diced

2 tablespoons chopped garlic

2 cups orange juice

1 cup lime juice

1 cup lemon juice

1½ teaspoons dried oregano

1 (2-to 3-pound) boneless venison roast

Kosher salt

Freshly ground black pepper

1. Place the onion, garlic, orange juice, lime juice, lemon juice, and oregano in a 6- to 8-quart slow cooker; stir to combine. Season the venison roast generously with salt and pepper, then place it in the slow cooker.

2. Cover and cook on High for 5 hours or on Low for 8 to 10 hours.

3. Use two forks to shred the meat right in the slow cooker, then mix well with the sauce. Serve immediately.

Pressure Cooker Variation: Follow step 1, combining all the ingredients in an electric pressure cooker. Lock the lid and close the steam valve. Select Manual and set the time for 60 minutes on High Pressure. Naturally release the steam for 15 to 20 minutes, then quick release any remaining steam. Pick up with step 3.

CHAPTER 4

SOUPS, STEWS, AND CHILIS

Soups and stews are the ultimate comfort foods, and both preparations are great ways to use those tough bits of venison you're not quite sure what to do with. From classic stews and chilis to a few new favorites, every recipe in this chapter is sure to please, especially during those chilly winter months.

VENISON RAMEN

Ramen was a major part of my diet during college, and it's still one of my favorite dishes. This is the easy wild game version that's a staple in my house. Pro tip: Freeze the backstrap for 30 to 45 minutes before slicing. When the meat is frozen, it's much easier to get thin slices.

Prep Time: 5 minutes
Cook Time: 15 minutes
Serves: 4

1 pound venison backstrap, cut into ⅛- to ¼-inch-thick slices

3 cups beef broth

¼ cup soy sauce

1 tablespoon minced garlic

1 tablespoon packed brown sugar

2 teaspoons minced or grated fresh ginger

2 teaspoons onion powder

1 teaspoon kosher salt

½ teaspoon freshly ground black pepper

1 cup frozen peas and carrots

3 (3-ounce) packages ramen noodles (noodles only; discard flavor packets)

Chopped scallions, sesame seeds, and sriracha sauce, for serving (optional)

1. In a large saucepan or Dutch oven, combine the venison, broth, soy sauce, garlic, brown sugar, ginger, onion powder, salt, and pepper. Bring the mixture to a boil over high heat, then let it boil for 2 minutes.

2. Add the frozen peas and carrots and ramen noodles. Continue to boil until the noodles are fully cooked, 3 to 5 minutes. Serve immediately with the toppings (if using).

VENISON POZOLE

SLOW COOKER | PRESSURE COOKER

Pozole is a traditional soup from Mexico that's a Christmas classic. In my family, however, we enjoy it year-round. A key ingredient in this soup is hominy, reconstituted dried corn kernels with the hulls and germs removed. Hominy adds a slightly nutty flavor and also absorbs many of the flavors of the soup. This family favorite is delicious with tortilla chips, either crumbled on top or used to dip in or scoop up the soup.

Prep Time: 10 minutes
Cook Time: 4 hours on High or
8 hours on Low
Serves: 6 to 8

1 large onion, diced

6 strips bacon, chopped

2 pounds venison stew meat

4 cups beef broth

¼ cup tomato paste

1 tablespoon minced garlic

1 tablespoon dried oregano

1½ teaspoons ground cumin

½ teaspoon ground cloves

½ teaspoon cayenne pepper
(optional)

1 (4-ounce) can chopped green
chiles, drained

1 (15-ounce) can
hominy, drained

Diced avocado, chopped fresh
cilantro, and lime wedges,
for serving

1. In a 6-quart slow cooker, combine the onion, bacon, venison, broth, tomato paste, garlic, oregano, cumin, cloves, cayenne (if using), and green chiles. Mix well.

2. Close the lid and cook on High for 4 hours or on Low for 8 hours. Thirty minutes before it's done, open the lid and stir in the hominy, then close the lid and continue cooking.

3. Top with avocado and cilantro, and serve with lime wedges.

Pressure Cooker Variation: In step 1, combine the ingredients in an electric pressure cooker. Lock the lid and close the steam valve. Select Manual and set the time for 25 minutes on High Pressure. Quick release the steam, then stir in the hominy. Close the lid and let the soup sit for 5 minutes or until the hominy is hot, then serve.

VENISON CHEESEBURGER SOUP

This recipe is a hunting camp must-have. I first made it completely by acci-dent with things that I found in the RV refrigerator. Someone said, "This tastes kind of like a Big Mac," so, "cheeseburger soup" it was. It's everything you want after hunting . . . or while binge watching your favorite shows.

Prep Time: 15 minutes
Cook Time: 30 minutes
Serves: 8

4 strips bacon, chopped

1 pound ground venison

1 large onion, diced

3 large russet potatoes, peeled and diced

2 celery stalks, diced

2 medium carrots, diced

1 (32-ounce) container chicken broth

2 teaspoons kosher salt

1 teaspoon freshly ground black pepper

1 teaspoon paprika

1 teaspoon dried basil

2 cups whole milk

3 cups shredded cheddar cheese

Chopped scallions, for garnish (optional)

1. In a 10-quart Dutch oven over medium-high heat, cook the bacon until most of the fat is rendered and the bacon is slightly crisp. Add the venison and onion. Cook until the ground meat is browned and the onion is translucent, 5 to 7 minutes.

2. Stir in the potatoes, celery, carrots, broth, salt, pepper, paprika, and basil. Bring to a simmer. Reduce the heat to medium-low, cover the pot, and simmer until the potatoes are tender, 10 to 12 minutes.

3. Stir in the milk, then stir in the cheese until well combined. Return the soup to a simmer, reduce the heat to low, and cook, uncovered, until the soup is thickened and well blended, about 5 minutes, being careful not to let it boil.

4. Serve immediately, garnished with scallions (if using).

VENISON ZUPPA TOSCANA WITH GNOCCHI

ONE POT

If you're a fan of the O.G. (yes, I'm talking about the Olive Garden) then you know how awesome this soup is. I'm not ashamed of it; Olive Garden was fine dining for my family when I was growing up, and this soup with bread sticks was a childhood favorite. It's creamy, meaty, studded with fluffy gnocchi, and is practically health food with the addition of kale.

Prep Time: 10 minutes
Cook Time: 30 minutes
Serves: 4 to 6

2 tablespoons olive oil

1 pound ground venison

1 medium onion, finely diced

2 garlic cloves, minced

1 teaspoon whole-grain mustard

1 teaspoon Italian seasoning

4 cups chicken broth

1 pound frozen or fresh potato gnocchi

1 small bunch kale or 1 pound spinach, trimmed and cut into bite-size pieces

1 cup heavy cream

Kosher salt

Freshly ground black pepper

Shaved Parmesan cheese, for garnish

1. Heat the olive oil in a large soup pot over medium-high heat, then add the ground venison. Cook, stirring with a wooden spoon to break the meat into small pieces, until the meat is no longer pink, about 5 minutes. Add the onion and cook until translucent, 4 to 5 minutes. Stir in the garlic, mustard, and Italian seasoning; cook for 1 minute.

2. Stir in the broth and gnocchi. Increase the heat to high, and bring the mixture to a boil. Reduce the heat to medium-low and simmer for 5 minutes.

3. Add the kale and cream and continue to simmer for about 10 minutes, until the gnocchi are cooked through. The gnocchi will release starch while they cook, thickening the broth; cook to your desired thickness. Season with salt and pepper to taste.

4. Garnish with the Parmesan and serve immediately.

CREAMY WILD RICE VENISON SOUP

ONE POT

This soup makes me long for sitting in a rocking chair in a cabin in the forest. Its earthy and savory, yet so easy to make, which is why it's a staple at hunting camp. I can easily transport the ingredients and whip it up in a flash. If you are going to make this at hunt camp, swap out the beef broth for water and 2 teaspoons beef bouillon granules. I also like to use mushrooms that I have foraged—any variety of edible mushrooms will do.

Prep Time: 15 minutes
Cook Time: 1 hour 20 minutes
Serves: 8 to 10

2 tablespoons vegetable oil

4 ounces mushrooms, chopped

1 pound ground venison

1 teaspoon Italian seasoning

6 cups beef broth, divided

3 celery stalks, finely diced

2 large onions, thinly sliced

1 carrot, finely diced

1 cup uncooked wild rice

1 tablespoon
   Worcestershire sauce

½ teaspoon freshly ground
   black pepper

½ teaspoon Tabasco (optional)

3 (10.75-ounce) cans
   condensed cream of
   mushroom soup

1. In a 5-quart Dutch oven over medium-high heat, combine the oil, mushrooms, ground venison, and Italian seasoning. Cook, stirring with a wooden spoon to break the meat into small pieces, until the meat is no longer pink, 5 to 7 minutes.

2. Add 2 cups of the broth, the celery, onions, carrot, wild rice, Worcestershire sauce, pepper, and Tabasco (if using). Bring to a boil. Reduce the heat to medium-low, cover, and simmer for 45 minutes.

3. Stir in the condensed soup and remaining 4 cups broth. Cover and let simmer for 30 minutes or until the rice is cooked.

COMFORTING VENISON STEW

ONE POT | SLOW COOKER | PRESSURE COOKER

This stew will have you looking forward to cold weather. It's my wild game take on a classic French dish. Red wine helps to break down the venison, creating extremely tender meat—all you'll need is a spoon. If you are like me and love homemade meals at the ready, freeze this stew for up to 3 months.

Prep Time: 15 minutes
Cook Time: 3 hours 45 minutes
Serves: 6

1½ pounds venison stew meat

1 tablespoon kosher salt

2 teaspoons freshly ground black pepper

¼ cup (½ stick) unsalted butter

2 tablespoons grapeseed oil or vegetable oil

3 medium onions, cut into 1-inch chunks

¼ cup balsamic vinegar

¼ cup tomato paste

3 tablespoons minced garlic

5 cups beef broth

2¾ cups dry red wine

3 tablespoons maple syrup

1 teaspoon dried thyme

8 ounces white button mushrooms, sliced

4 large carrots, cut on the diagonal into 1-inch-thick pieces

1½ pounds Yukon Gold potatoes, cut into bite-size pieces

1 cup frozen peas

1. Set a rack in the middle position of the oven. Preheat the oven to 325°F. Pat the venison cubes dry with a paper towel, then season them with the salt and pepper.

2. Heat the butter and oil in a large Dutch oven over medium-high heat until the butter melts. Add one-third of the meat and cook until it is browned on all sides, about 5 minutes. Transfer to a plate and repeat with the remaining meat.

3. Add the onions and vinegar to the pot. Using a wooden spoon, scrape the brown bits off the bottom of the pot. Cook until the onions are lightly browned, about 5 minutes. Stir in the tomato paste and garlic and cook, stirring, for 2 minutes. Return the venison and any accumulated juices to the pot. Stir in the broth, wine, maple syrup, and thyme. Bring to a boil. Remove from the heat, cover, and transfer to the oven. Braise for 2 hours.

4. Remove the pot from the oven and stir in the mushrooms, carrots, and potatoes. Cover and braise in the oven for 1 hour.

5. Stir in the frozen peas, cover the pot, and braise in the oven for 30 minutes.

Slow Cooker Variation: After browning the meat in step 2, transfer it to a 6- to 8-quart slow cooker and add all the remaining ingredients except the peas. Cover and cook on High for 5 hours or on Low for 8 to 10 hours. Thirty minutes before the stew is finished cooking, stir in the peas. Cover and continue cooking.

Pressure Cooker Variation: Select Sauté and sear the venison in the butter and olive oil as directed in step 1 in an electric pressure cooker. Add all the other ingredients except the peas, lock the lid, and close the steam valve. Select Manual and set the time for 35 minutes on High Pressure. Quick release the steam and stir in the peas. Close the lid and let sit for 5 minutes until the peas are hot.

VENISON CARBONNADE STEW WITH EGG NOODLES

SLOW COOKER | PRESSURE COOKER

Carbonnade is a Flemish beef stew that gets its flavor from the use of Belgian abbey-style ale. It is deeply satisfying and perfect for a cool winter's night. I like to serve it over egg noodles, but give mashed potatoes a try, too.

Prep Time: 15 minutes
Cook Time: 5 hours on High or 8 to 10 hours on Low
Serves: 8 to 10

1 tablespoon unsalted butter

1 tablespoon olive oil

3 pounds venison stew meat

1 large onion, diced

1 tablespoon minced garlic

2 cups beef broth, divided

2 cups Belgian abbey-style ale

2 tablespoons apple cider vinegar

1½ tablespoons Dijon mustard

1 tablespoon packed brown sugar

1 teaspoon dried tarragon

1 teaspoon kosher salt

½ teaspoon freshly ground black pepper

1 bay leaf

12 ounces extra-wide egg noodles

1. In a large skillet over high heat, melt the butter with the oil. Add half the venison and sear until browned on all sides, about 3 minutes. Transfer the seared meat to a 6- to 8-quart slow cooker, then repeat with the remaining venison.

2. Add the onion, garlic, 1¾ cups broth, the ale, vinegar, mustard, sugar, tarragon, salt, pepper, and bay leaf; stir to combine.

3. Cover and cook on High for 5 hours or on Low for 8 to 10 hours.

4. Thirty minutes before the stew is finished cooking, bring a large pot of water to a boil and cook the egg noodles according to the package directions. Drain.

5. Remove the bay leaf. Serve the beef stew over the egg noodles.

Pressure Cooker Variation: Select Sauté and sear the venison in the butter and olive oil as directed in step 1. Add all the other ingredients except the noodles, lock the lid, and close the steam valve. Select Manual and set the time for 35 minutes on High Pressure. Naturally release the steam for 15 to 20 minutes, then quick release any remaining steam. Prepare the noodles as in step 4 during the natural release time.

VENISON CHILE VERDE

SLOW COOKER | PRESSURE COOKER

Chile verde is one of my favorite stews. As a chef, I used to take time to char each chile and simmer for hours. But then life happened, and I came up with this ultra-easy version that is equally as good. I like to double the batch so I can freeze some for later.

Prep Time: 5 minutes
Cook Time: 4 hours on High or 8 hours on Low
Serves: 8

2 pounds venison stew meat

1 large onion, diced

2 tablespoons minced garlic

2 (16-ounce) jars green salsa

3 cups chicken broth

1 (4-ounce) can chopped green chiles, drained

2 teaspoons ground cumin

2 teaspoons kosher salt

1 teaspoon freshly ground black pepper

Cooked white rice (optional), for serving

Shredded Monterey Jack cheese, sour cream, and chopped fresh cilantro, for serving

1. Combine the venison, onion, garlic, salsa, broth, green chiles, cumin, salt, and pepper in a 6- to 8-quart slow cooker. Stir well.

2. Close the lid and cook on High for 4 hours or on Low for 8 hours.

3. Serve the soup ladled over rice (if using), and offer bowls of cheese, sour cream, and cilantro at the table.

Pressure Cooker Variation: In step 1, combine all the ingredients (except the rice and toppings) in an electric pressure cooker. Lock the lid and close the steam valve. Select Manual and set the time for 35 minutes on High Pressure. Naturally release the steam for 10 minutes, then quick release any remaining steam.

EVERYTHING-BUT-THE-KITCHEN-SINK CHILI

SLOW COOKER

Here's a great dish to clear out your refrigerator or pantry; it uses just about everything you might have on hand. Feel free to substitute any beans and add any canned or frozen vegetables, such as frozen peas and carrots. It will still taste fabulous. Just don't go throwing in that can of anchovies you have no idea why you bought!

Prep Time: 10 minutes
Cook Time: 4 hours on High or 8 to 10 hours on Low
Serves: 12

1 tablespoon unsalted butter

1 tablespoon olive oil

1 pound ground venison

1 pound venison stew meat

1 large onion, diced

1 (32-ounce) container beef broth

1 (28-ounce) can crushed tomatoes

1 (4-ounce) can chopped green chiles, drained

1 (15.25-ounce) can corn kernels, drained

1 (15.5-ounce) can black beans, drained and rinsed

1 (15.5-ounce) can chili beans

1 (1.25-ounce) packet chili seasoning

Shredded cheddar cheese, chopped scallions, chopped jalapeños, and corn chips, for serving

1. In a large skillet over medium-high heat, melt the butter with the olive oil. Add the ground meat and cook, breaking it up with a wooden spoon into small crumbles, until no longer pink, about 5 minutes.

2. Transfer the cooked ground meat to a 6- to 8-quart slow cooker, and add the stew meat, onion, broth, tomatoes, green chiles, corn, black beans, chili beans, and chili seasoning.

3. Cover and cook on High for 4 hours or on Low for 8 to 10 hours.

4. Serve with bowls of cheddar cheese, scallions, jalapeños, and corn chips at the table.

QUICK AND EASY CHIPOTLE CHILI

SLOW COOKER | PRESSURE COOKER

Chipotles are smoked ripe jalapeños. You can buy them dried or canned in adobo sauce. If you're a spicy person and like to turn up the heat, add more chipotles. If you're not as adventurous, use one chipotle instead of two.

Prep Time: 5 minutes
Cook Time: 25 minutes on High Pressure, plus 15 minutes natural release
Serves: 8

2 pounds ground venison

8 strips bacon, chopped

1 large onion, diced

1 (14.5-ounce) can fire-roasted tomatoes

1 (6-ounce) can tomato paste

2 cups beef broth

2 canned chipotle chiles in adobo sauce, chopped, plus 1 tablespoon adobo sauce from the can

2 tablespoons minced garlic

1 tablespoon ground cumin

2 teaspoons kosher salt

Freshly ground black pepper

1 (15-ounce) can black beans, drained and rinsed

1 (15-ounce) can kidney beans, drained and rinsed

Shredded cheddar cheese, sour cream, sliced jalapeños, and chopped fresh cilantro, for serving

1. Place the venison, bacon, and onion in a 6- to 8-quart electric pressure cooker and select Sauté. Cook, breaking the venison into crumbles, for 10 minutes or until the meat is no longer pink. Add the tomatoes, tomato paste, broth, chipotles and sauce, garlic, cumin, salt, and pepper. Stir to combine.

2. Lock the lid and close the steam valve. Select Manual and set the time for 15 minutes on High Pressure.

3. When the timer sounds, naturally release the steam for about 15 minutes, then quick release any remaining steam.

4. Open the pressure cooker and stir in the beans. Put the cover back on and let the chili sit for about 3 minutes, until the beans are hot.

5. Serve with bowls of cheese, sour cream, jalapeños, and cilantro at the table.

Slow Cooker Variation: Cook the bacon in a skillet until it is almost crispy, then add the venison and cook until it is no longer pink, about 5 minutes. Add the bacon and ground meat to a large slow cooker, along with all the remaining ingredients (except the toppings), and stir to combine. Cover and cook on High for 4 hours or on Low for 8 hours.

CHAPTER 5

GROUND MEAT MAGIC

Ground meat is the most common cut of venison, and its possibilities are endless; it's a great way to utilize tough cuts that aren't good enough to eat on their own. Plus, ground meat also allows you to get delicious meals on your table fast. If you are making dishes with ground venison and finding them to be quite dry, it's because you're not adding enough fat. Add a tablespoon of duck fat, bacon fat, or lard to the ground meat while cooking to solve your dry meat problem.

VENISON TOT-CHOS

6-INGREDIENT | 30-MINUTE

Tater tot nachos came about in my early college graduate years, when I couldn't afford much and practically lived on cheap wine and Cheez Whiz. While my personal tater tot nachos have gotten some upgrades since then— Parmesan cheese, steak bits, drizzles of truffle oil—now that I have a child, I am not ashamed to admit that this quick and easy version is a staple in my house.

Prep Time: 5 minutes
Cook Time: 15 minutes
Serves: 4 to 6

1 (28-ounce) bag frozen tater tots

1 pound ground venison

⅔ cup water

¼ cup taco seasoning

1 cup shredded Mexican cheese blend

½ cup salsa

¼ cup sour cream

1. Preheat the oven to 425°F.

2. Spread the frozen tater tots on a baking sheet. Bake for 10 to 12 minutes, until the outsides of the tots are golden and crispy.

3. While the tots bake, heat a large nonstick skillet over medium-high heat and add the ground venison. Using a wooden spoon, break up the meat into little crumbles as it cooks. When the meat is no longer pink, add the water and taco seasoning and gently stir until the seasoning is fully incorporated. Cook until most of the water has evaporated and a sauce has formed.

4. Remove the tots from the oven and place them on a large ovenproof serving platter. Top the tots with the ground meat, then sprinkle with the cheese. Bake for 1 to 2 minutes, until the cheese melts.

5. Top with the salsa and sour cream, and serve immediately.

VENISON SLOPPY JOE BOMBS

Mom life has made me super creative when it comes to feeding the little one, sneaking vegetables in where I can and making things fun so they will actually want to eat them. Recently, we took a family trip to D.C. and had bagel bombs from a well-known bakery. They were so fun to eat and delicious that my little one ate three. So, now I turn anything into a "bomb." (These sloppy joe pouches are great for football parties, too.)

Prep Time: 20 minutes
Cook Time: 25 minutes
Serves: 6

Nonstick cooking spray

2 tablespoons unsalted butter

1 pound ground venison

1 small onion, diced

½ cup ketchup

1½ teaspoons garlic powder

1½ teaspoons chili powder

½ teaspoon mustard powder

3 (8-ounce) tubes crescent rolls or crescent roll sheets

6 tablespoons sloppy joe mix, divided

½ cup shredded cheddar cheese

¼ cup melted unsalted butter

Everything bagel seasoning (optional)

1. Preheat the oven to 350°F. Coat a 12-cup muffin pan with cooking spray.

2. In a large skillet over medium-high heat, melt the butter. Add the venison and onion, and use a wooden spoon to break the meat up into small crumbles. Cook until the meat is no longer pink, about 5 minutes. Stir in the ketchup, garlic powder, chili powder, and mustard powder; cook for 1 more minute, then remove the skillet from the heat.

3. Place the crescent rolls or sheets on a clean work surface. If using rolls, pinch the perforated lines together. Using a rolling pin, gently roll out the dough to an even ¼-inch thickness. Using a 4-inch round cookie cutter, make 12 circles.

4. Place 1 tablespoon of the sloppy joe mix in the center of each circle, and top with 2 teaspoons of the cheese. Dab your finger with water, and wet the edges of the dough circles. Bring up all the edges to make a small pouch, and pinch to seal.

5. Place the bombs in the prepared muffin pan. Use a pastry brush to brush the tops with the melted butter. Sprinkle with the bagel seasoning (if using). Bake for 15 to 17 minutes, until golden brown. Serve immediately.

VENISON PATTY MELTS

A patty melt is the best of both worlds—a burger and a hot, cheesy sandwich. The addition of wine to the onions takes this to a whole new level. In my house, these are the ultimate Friday-night cheat meal. I love to serve them with sweet potato fries topped with some of the caramelized onions.

Prep Time: 10 minutes
Cook Time: 50 minutes
Serves: 5

9 tablespoons unsalted butter, divided

2 large onions, sliced

2 teaspoons kosher salt, divided, plus more to taste

¼ cup white wine or 3 tablespoons white wine vinegar

2 pounds ground venison

1 tablespoon Dijon mustard

1 teaspoon dried thyme

1 teaspoon garlic powder

1 teaspoon onion powder

½ teaspoon freshly ground black pepper

2 tablespoons vegetable oil

10 slices Texas toast or thick-cut white bread

5 slices American cheese

1. In a medium skillet over medium-high heat, melt 3 tablespoons of the butter. Add the onions and 1 teaspoon of salt and cook, stirring often, until golden, about 10 minutes. Add the wine and continue to cook until the onions are caramelized and the wine has evaporated, 5 to 8 minutes. Remove the skillet from the heat.

2. In a large bowl, combine the venison, mustard, thyme, garlic powder, onion powder, pepper, and the remaining 1 teaspoon salt, using your hands to mix well. Form into 5 patties.

3. Heat the oil in a large cast-iron skillet over medium-high heat until hot. Working in batches if necessary, add the patties and cook for 3 to 4 minutes per side, until they are browned and their internal temperature reaches 160°F. Transfer the patties to a plate, and repeat with the remaining patties.

4. In the same skillet, melt 2 tablespoons of butter. Add 2 slices of bread to the pan, and top each with a patty, some caramelized onions, and a slice of cheese. Cap with a piece of bread. Cook until the bottom of the bread is golden brown, 1 to 1½ minutes. Then gently flip and cook until golden brown, 1 to 1½ minutes. Repeat, adding more butter to the pan, to make 5 sandwiches. Serve immediately.

VENISON PIZZA CALZONES

These venison calzones are like a grown-up, sophisticated version of those savory pastry pockets we all loved as kids. I like to make large versions, as in this recipe, or individual ones that I can freeze and reheat later. Get creative—add veggies or try different cheeses. Use Alfredo sauce and add some broccoli with the ground venison.

Prep Time: 10 minutes
Cook Time: 30 minutes
Serves: 4 to 6

3 tablespoons olive oil, divided

1 pound ground venison

1 cup store-bought pizza sauce

½ cup chopped pepperoni

1 pound store-bought
   pizza dough

1 cup shredded low-moisture
   mozzarella cheese

Kosher salt

1. Preheat the oven to 450°F. Grease a baking sheet lightly with olive oil.

2. Heat 2 tablespoons of the oil in a medium skillet over medium-high heat until hot. Add the venison and cook, using a wooden spoon to break the meat into small crumbles, until it is no longer pink, about 5 minutes. Remove the skillet from the heat and stir in the pizza sauce and pepperoni.

3. On a lightly floured work surface, divide the pizza dough into two equal pieces. Roll out each piece into an 8-inch circle that is about ¼ inch thick. Spoon half of the meat mixture in the center of each circle, and sprinkle with half the cheese. Wet your finger with water, and lightly dampen half of the edge of each dough circle. Fold the dough over in half, and crimp the edges to seal. Repeat.

4. Place the calzones on the prepared baking sheet. Using a pastry brush, brush the tops with the remaining 1 tablespoon of oil and sprinkle with a little bit of salt. Use a sharp paring knife to make two 1-inch-long slits in the top of each calzone.

5. Bake for 20 to 25 minutes or until the calzones are golden brown. Let cool for about 5 minutes before serving. Cut each calzone in half or thirds to serve.

VENISON POTPIE

You don't need a special occasion to make potpie, but it certainly is occasion worthy. Venison is earthy and rich in flavor, which makes it perfect for classic potpie. If you are feeling extra special, double the piecrust amount and use a muffin pan to make individual potpies—just be sure to parbake the bottoms of the pies in the pan for 10 minutes before filling them.

Prep Time: 10 minutes
Cook Time: 1 hour 10 minutes
Serves: 8

⅓ cup (5⅓ tablespoons) unsalted butter

1 pound ground venison

1 medium onion, chopped

⅓ cup all-purpose flour

2 cups chicken broth

½ cup chopped celery

1 (12- to 13-ounce) bag frozen peas and carrots

⅔ cup heavy cream

1½ teaspoons kosher salt

1 teaspoon freshly ground black pepper

1 teaspoon dried rosemary

½ teaspoon dried sage (optional)

2 (9-inch) homemade or refrigerated piecrusts

1 egg, beaten

1. Preheat the oven to 375°F.

2. Melt the butter in a large saucepan over medium-high heat. Add the venison and onion and cook until the venison is cooked through and the onion is golden brown, about 5 minutes. Whisk in the flour and cook for 1 minute. Gradually whisk in the broth, about ¼ cup at a time, until smooth.

3. Stir in the celery, peas and carrots, cream, salt, pepper, rosemary, and sage (if using). Cook, stirring occasionally, for about 20 minutes.

4. Meanwhile, roll out one of the piecrusts to a roughly 10- to 12-inch circle. Carefully fit the dough into a 9-inch pie plate, gently pressing it into the bottom; transfer the pie plate to the oven and bake for 5 minutes.

5. Remove the crust from the oven and pour in the filling. Roll out the remaining pie dough to a roughly 10-inch circle. Transfer the dough to the top of the filled piecrust and crimp to seal the edges. Cut three small slits in the top of the crust for ventilation.

6. Using a pastry brush, brush the egg over the top of the crust. Bake until the top crust is golden brown, about 40 minutes.

ELOTE CASSEROLE WITH TACO-SPICED VENISON

ONE POT

You haven't lived if you haven't had elote, also known as Mexican street corn. Sold by vendors, it is char-grilled corn on the cob that's coated in a creamy mixture and sprinkled with spices, cilantro, lime juice, and cotija cheese. It's absolutely delicious. I took my love for elote and made it into a casserole—it may just be the best dish you ever take to a BBQ or potluck.

Prep Time: 10 minutes
Cook Time: 55 minutes
Serves: 8 to 10

¼ cup olive oil

1 pound ground venison

½ cup water

3 tablespoons taco seasoning

2 (12- to 14.4-ounce) bags frozen corn kernels, thawed

⅓ cup sour cream

¼ cup mayonnaise

1 tablespoon lime juice

Kosher salt

Freshly ground black pepper

4 ounces cotija cheese, crumbled, or Parmesan cheese, grated

2 tablespoons chopped fresh cilantro

1. Preheat the oven to 350°F.

2. Heat the olive oil in a medium cast-iron skillet over medium-high heat until hot. Add the venison and cook, using a wooden spoon to break it into small pieces, until the meat is no longer pink, about 5 minutes.

3. Add the water and taco seasoning and cook, stirring to coat, until the water has evaporated, 2 to 3 minutes. Remove the pan from the heat.

4. In a large bowl, stir together the corn, sour cream, mayonnaise, and lime juice. Season with salt and black pepper to taste. Stir in half the cheese. Add this mixture to the skillet and stir to combine with the venison. Transfer the skillet to the oven.

5. Bake until bubbly and heated through, 30 to 40 minutes. Sprinkle with the remaining cheese and the cilantro. Serve immediately.

BACON-WRAPPED VENISON MEAT LOAF

Venison is naturally much leaner than beef, so it's best when cooked with added fat. We all know everything is better with bacon, but in this recipe, the bacon is used for both its delicious, smoky flavor and its fat content. I make this super easy meat loaf with ketchup, but try it with your favorite BBQ sauce, too. It's great with mashed potatoes or steamed vegetables.

Prep Time: 15 minutes
Cook Time: 1 hour
Serves: 4

1½ pounds ground venison

1 small onion, diced

1 cup grated Parmesan cheese

1 large egg

¼ cup ketchup or BBQ sauce

6 strips bacon

1. Preheat the oven to 350°F.

2. In a large bowl, combine the venison, onion, Parmesan, egg, and ketchup; use your hands to mix well. Transfer the meat mixture to a 9-by-13-inch baking pan, and shape it into a loaf that is about 2 inches tall. Arrange the bacon slices over the loaf.

3. Bake for 1 hour or until the internal temperature of the meat loaf reaches 160°F.

4. Remove the meat loaf from the oven. Let it rest for 5 minutes before serving.

VENISON SHEPHERD'S PIE

Did you know that shepherd's pie is not a simple country dish, but a classic French one? It was created by Antoine-Augustin Parmentier, who was instrumental in promoting the potato in France during the eighteenth century. Many potato dishes, including potato and leek soup, have been attributed to him. To make this recipe even easier, top the meat mixture with frozen tater tots instead of mashed potatoes.

Prep Time: 10 minutes
Cook Time: 45 minutes
Serves: 6

1½ pounds russet potatoes, peeled and cubed

¾ cup sour cream

¼ cup (½ stick) unsalted butter

Kosher salt

Freshly ground black pepper

1 tablespoon vegetable oil

1 medium onion, diced

1 tablespoon chopped garlic

1 pound ground venison

2½ cups frozen mixed vegetables

2 tablespoons all-purpose flour

½ cup beef broth

½ teaspoon dried thyme

1. Preheat the oven to 400°F.

2. Bring a large pot of water to a boil. Add the potatoes and cook until tender, 12 to 14 minutes, then drain and return them to the pot. Add the sour cream and butter, and mash the potatoes until they are smooth and creamy. Season with salt and pepper to taste.

3. Heat the oil in a large cast-iron skillet over medium-high heat. When the oil is hot, add the onion and cook, stirring, until translucent, about 4 minutes. Add the garlic and cook for 1 minute. Add the venison and, using a wooden spoon, break up the meat into small crumbles. Cook until the meat is no longer pink, about 5 minutes. Add the frozen mixed vegetables, corn, flour, broth, and thyme, and season with salt and pepper to taste. Stir until combined. Cook, stirring, until the mixture has thickened to a saucy consistency, 4 to 5 minutes. Remove the skillet from the heat.

4. Gently spread the mashed potatoes in an even layer over the meat mixture. Bake for 20 to 25 minutes or until the potatoes are golden brown on top. Serve immediately.

VENISON BOLOGNESE

Bolognese is hands down my favorite pasta dish. It's simple to master, yet there are so many versions. While in Italy, I noticed that the Italian way of making Bolognese is to go light on the sauce. This meat sauce calls for just a little tomato paste, which I find to be wonderful.

Prep Time: 15 minutes
Cook Time: 2 hours
Serves: 6

5 strips bacon, minced

3 celery stalks, finely diced

2 large onions, finely diced

1 large carrot, finely diced

2 pounds ground venison

1½ teaspoons kosher salt

½ teaspoon ground nutmeg

½ teaspoon ground cinnamon

¼ teaspoon red pepper flakes (optional)

1½ cups dry white wine

4 cups beef broth

¼ cup tomato paste

2 bay leaves

1 pound fettuccine pasta

1 cup heavy cream

1½ cups grated Parmesan cheese, divided

1. Cook the bacon in a large Dutch oven over medium-high heat until it just starts to crisp, 3 to 4 minutes. Add the celery, onions, and carrot and cook, stirring constantly, until the vegetables are lightly golden, 8 to 10 minutes.

2. Add the venison, stirring with a wooden spoon to crumble the meat. Add the salt, nutmeg, cinnamon, and red pepper flakes (if using). Cook, stirring, until the meat is lightly browned, 3 to 4 minutes. Add the wine and cook, scraping up any browned bits from the bottom of the pan, until almost all the wine has evaporated, about 3 minutes.

3. Add the broth, tomato paste, and bay leaves, and cook until the broth has reduced by half, about 10 minutes. Reduce the heat to low, cover, and simmer for 1½ to 2 hours, stirring occasionally.

4. Twenty minutes before the sauce is done, bring a large pot of water to a boil, and cook the fettuccine according to the package directions.

5. Remove the bay leaves from the sauce, then stir in the cream and half the Parmesan. Ladle the sauce over the fettuccine and serve sprinkled with the remaining Parmesan.

Pressure Cooker Variation: Select Sauté and cook the bacon, vegetables, and venison as directed in steps 1 and 2 in an electric pressure cooker. Add all the other ingredients except the pasta, cream, and cheese. Lock the lid and close the steam valve. Select Manual and set the time for 25 minutes on High Pressure. Naturally release the steam for 15 to 20 minutes, then quick release any remaining steam. Prepare the fettuccine as directed in step 4 during the natural release time. Pick up with step 5.

VENISON LASAGNA

I love making lasagna, but it can be quite laborious, and when I do make it, my poor family ends up eating it all week. So, I created a weekday version—with no-boil noodles and minimal ingredients—that comes together in minutes. This delicious lasagna makes great leftovers, too.

Prep Time: 10 minutes
Cook Time: 45 minutes
Serves: 6

Nonstick cooking spray

2 tablespoons olive oil

1 pound ground venison

Kosher salt

Freshly ground black pepper

1 tablespoon Italian seasoning

1 cup ricotta cheese

1 large egg

2 cups store-bought
marinara sauce

1 (9-ounce) box oven-ready
lasagna noodles

1 cup shredded low-moisture
mozzarella cheese

½ cup shredded
Parmesan cheese

1. Preheat the oven to 350°F. Coat a 9-by-13-inch baking dish with nonstick cooking spray.

2. Heat the oil in a medium skillet over medium-high heat until hot. Add the venison and salt and pepper to taste, and stir with a wooden spoon to break the meat into small crumbles. Cook until the meat is no longer pink, about 5 minutes. Stir in the Italian seasoning, then remove the skillet from the heat.

3. In a medium bowl, stir together the ricotta and egg until smooth.

4. Spread about 2 tablespoons of the marinara on the bottom of the prepared pan. Break the lasagna noodles so you create one layer of lasagna noodles covering the bottom. Layer ¼ to ½ cup of the meat mixture over the noodles. Drizzle the top of the meat with some of the marinara. Dollop about ¼ cup of the ricotta mixture evenly over the marinara, sprinkle with a bit of the mozzarella, and then arrange another layer of the noodles on top. Repeat this layering until you reach the top of the pan. When the pan is filled, sprinkle the top with the Parmesan.

5. Bake for 45 minutes. Let the lasagna rest for 5 minutes before serving.

VENISON ENCHILADA CASSEROLE

This was a childhood favorite of mine, and now that I'm a mom, I serve it to my little one often. I frequently try to sneak some veggies into the dish by adding a layer of sliced zucchini or squash—kids will never know. This casserole is delicious as is, but it's especially tasty topped with diced avocado, chopped scallions, and a dollop of sour cream.

Prep Time: 10 minutes
Cook Time: 35 minutes
Serves: 6

Nonstick cooking spray

1 pound ground venison

1 (19-ounce) can red enchilada sauce

1 (15.25-ounce) can corn kernels, drained

1 (15-ounce) can pinto beans, drained and rinsed

1 (4.5-ounce) can chopped green chiles, drained

12 corn tortillas

2 cups shredded Mexican cheese blend

1. Preheat the oven to 350°F. Coat a 9-by-11-inch baking dish with nonstick cooking spray.

2. In a large skillet over medium-high heat, cook the venison, using a wooden spoon to break it up into small crumbles, until the meat is no longer pink, about 5 minutes. Add the enchilada sauce, corn, beans, and chiles and stir to combine. Remove the skillet from the heat.

3. Arrange 4 tortillas on the bottom of the prepared pan. Spread half the meat mixture evenly over the tortillas. Top with about one-third of the cheese. Arrange another 4 tortillas over the cheese. Spread with the remaining meat mixture, sprinkle with another third of the cheese, top with the remaining tortillas, and sprinkle with the remaining cheese.

4. Cover the pan with foil and bake for 30 minutes or until cooked through and bubbling along the edges. Serve immediately.

CHAPTER 6

GRILLING AND SMOKING

This chapter is for grilling and smoker enthusiasts! Here, you'll find classic grilled meat dishes—burgers, steaks, kebabs—without a lot of fuss. Many of them are ready in 30 minutes or less. Additionally, there are several recipes to smoke venison, which results in succulent and perfectly moist and tender meat every time. New to smoking meat? No worries, I will walk you through each step for stellar results every time.

VENISON BUTTER BURGERS

If you are from the Midwest, then you know what a butter burger is. If you're not, you are about to fall in love with this Midwestern favorite. I believe the butter burger gets its name from buttering the buns, but I take it to another level by adding grated frozen butter to the ground meat for extra buttery goodness. If you're planning to make this recipe, throw a stick of butter in the freezer ahead of time.

Prep Time: 15 minutes
Cook Time: 10 minutes
Serves: 4

1 pound ground venison

1 teaspoon kosher salt

½ teaspoon freshly ground black pepper

½ teaspoon garlic powder

½ cup (1 stick) unsalted butter, frozen

2 tablespoons vegetable oil

4 slices American cheese

4 hamburger buns

3 tablespoons unsalted butter, softened

Dill pickles, sliced tomatoes, iceberg lettuce, mayonnaise, ketchup, and/or mustard, for serving

1. Preheat an outdoor grill to 400°F.

2. In a large bowl, combine the venison, salt, pepper, and garlic powder. Using the large holes of a box grater, grate the frozen butter into the ground meat. Using a wooden spoon, quickly stir to combine. Divide the mixture into 4 patties.

3. Brush the oil on the grill grates. Place the patties on the grates over direct heat, close the lid, and grill for 4 minutes on each side or until the internal temperature of the burgers reaches 145°F (for medium), or cook the burgers to your desired degree of doneness. Top each burger with a slice of cheese, let the cheese melt, and then transfer the burgers to a plate.

4. While the burgers are cooking, spread the cut sides of the buns with the softened butter. Place the buttered side of the buns over indirect heat, and cook for 1 minute or until toasted. Remove the buns from the grill.

5. To assemble, place each bottom bun on a plate, top with a patty and any desired toppings, and cap with the top bun. Serve immediately.

GRILLING & SMOKING TIPS

Grilling is one of my favorite ways to cook venison. Here are a few pointers:

When you grill, you will either be cooking right over the fire (direct heat) or away from the flames (indirect heat).

➤ If cooking entirely over direct heat, pour the charcoal in and light it up. For a gas grill, fire up all the burners with the lid closed for 15 minutes to preheat before cooking.

➤ If you need an indirect fire for all or some of your cook time, for a charcoal fire, get your coals burning, then push them to one side so you have a portion of the grill that is free of flames—that is where your meat will go when the recipe says to use indirect heat. For a gas grill, preheat it with all the burners on and the lid closed. When you are ready to cook, turn off half of the burners; that side of the grill will be your indirect-heat spot.

As for smoking, all of my recipes are written for an electric smoker, since that is what I use at home. If you don't have an electric smoker, you can use a charcoal grill with an indirect setup instead. Once you've got your fire going, add wood chunks and close the lid until the grill is filled with smoke, then place the venison in the indirect-heat spot away from the coals. I like to put an aluminum tray filled with water underneath the meat to help regulate the temperature.

If you're smoking meat low and slow for a number of hours, you will need to replenish the coals. The best way is to add unlit charcoal, briquettes, or wood chunks to your grill or smoker when the temperature starts dropping. The lit coals will light the fresh fuel and keep the fire going. If the temperature in the grill gets too high, close the vents to reduce the amount of oxygen, which will lower the temperature.

VENISON MUSHROOM BURGERS WITH UMAMI SAUCE

Get ready for a unique burger jam-packed with rich, savory umami flavor. If you're a fan of cheeseburgers, add a slice of fontina cheese. This recipe makes extra sauce; I like to use it on sandwiches and as a dip for French fries and roasted veggies.

Prep Time: 15 minutes, plus 30 minutes soaking time
Cook Time: 10 minutes
Serves: 4

2 ounces dried shiitake mushrooms

1 cup mayonnaise

¼ cup grated Parmesan cheese

1 tablespoon Dijon mustard

1 teaspoon Worcestershire sauce

1 pound ground venison

1 tablespoon soy sauce

2 teaspoons garlic powder

1 teaspoon onion powder

½ teaspoon freshly ground black pepper

4 large portobello mushrooms, stemmed

2 tablespoons unsalted butter, melted

4 potato buns

1. Place the shiitakes in a small heatproof bowl and cover with hot water; let soak until softened, about 30 minutes. Drain, rinse the mushrooms, and mince. Wipe the bowl clean. Return the minced shiitakes to the bowl, add the mayonnaise, Parmesan, mustard, and Worcestershire sauce, and stir to combine.

2. Preheat an outdoor grill to 400°F.

3. In a large bowl, combine the venison, soy sauce, garlic powder, onion powder, and pepper. Use your hands to mix everything together. Form the mixture into 4 patties.

4. Brush the portobello mushroom caps with the melted butter.

5. Place the mushroom caps and venison patties on the grill over direct heat and close the lid. Grill the mushroom caps, turning once, until soft and slightly charred, 5 to 6 minutes. Grill the burgers to your desired degree of doneness, about 4 minutes per side for medium rare.

6. To assemble the burgers, slather the sauce on the cut sides of the buns. Place each bottom bun on a plate, then top with a patty, grilled mushroom cap, and a top bun. Serve immediately.

CHILI-RUBBED GRILLED BACKSTRAP

This backstrap packs a punch with just the right amount of heat and spice. It's a beautiful example of how you can harness a ton of flavor from minimal ingredients. If you want to go all out, serve this with my Blue Cheese Sauce (page 73).

Prep Time: 15 minutes
Cook Time: 15 minutes
Serves: 6

1 tablespoon garlic salt
2 teaspoons chili powder
1 teaspoon ground cumin
½ teaspoon ground allspice
¼ teaspoon cayenne pepper
1 (2-pound) venison backstrap

1. Preheat the grill to 400°F, setting it up for indirect cooking (see page 70).

2. In a small bowl, combine the garlic salt, chili powder, cumin, allspice, and cayenne; mix well.

3. Trim any silver skin or excess fat off the backstrap. Sprinkle the seasoning mixture evenly on all sides of the meat.

4. Place the backstrap on the grill over direct heat, close the lid, and sear the meat for 2 to 3 minutes per side. Move the meat to indirect heat, close the lid, and cook until the internal temperature of the meat reaches 130°F (for rare), 5 to 8 minutes, or cook the meat to your desired degree of doneness.

5. Transfer the backstrap to a cutting board and let it rest for 5 minutes. Slice and serve.

GRILLED BACKSTRAP WITH BLUE CHEESE SAUCE

6-INGREDIENT | 30-MINUTE

Sometimes you deserve a steak house meal during the week. After all, self-care is important, right? Well, this recipe is so easy that you might want to make it more than once a week. All this dish needs to make it a meal is creamy mashed potatoes or some roasted asparagus on the side.

Prep Time: 15 minutes
Cook Time: 15 minutes
Serves: 6

½ cup heavy cream

⅓ cup crumbled blue cheese

2 tablespoons unsalted butter

1 teaspoon lemon juice

1 teaspoon
  Worcestershire sauce

1 (2-pound) venison backstrap

Kosher salt

Freshly ground black pepper

1. Preheat an outdoor grill to 400°F, setting it up for indirect cooking (see page 70).

2. In a medium saucepan over medium heat, combine the cream, blue cheese, butter, lemon juice, and Worcestershire sauce. Cook, stirring constantly, until the butter and cheese are melted and the sauce is smooth, 5 to 6 minutes. Turn the heat to very low to keep the sauce warm; don't let it boil.

3. Season the backstrap generously with salt and pepper. Place the backstrap on the grill over direct heat, close the lid, and sear for 2 to 3 minutes per side. Move the meat to indirect heat, close the lid, and cook until the internal temperature of the meat reaches 130°F (for rare), 5 to 8 minutes, or grill the meat to your desired degree of doneness.

4. Transfer the backstrap to a cutting board. Let it rest for 5 minutes, then slice and serve.

BACON-WRAPPED VENISON MEDALLIONS WITH RED WINE COMPOUND BUTTER

6 INGREDIENT

Compound butter is no more complicated than adding flavorful ingredients like chopped fresh herbs to softened butter. This simple red wine compound butter is stunning, easy, and delicious.

Prep Time: 15 minutes, plus 1 hour to chill
Cook Time: 10 minutes
Serves: 4

¼ cup dark red wine

1 tablespoon minced garlic

½ cup (1 stick) unsalted butter, softened

1 teaspoon chopped fresh rosemary

1 teaspoon kosher salt, plus more to taste

½ teaspoon freshly ground black pepper, plus more to taste

4 strips hickory-smoked bacon

4 (1½-inch-thick) venison medallions

1. In a small saucepan, combine the wine and garlic. Bring to a boil over medium-high heat, and continue to boil until reduced by half, 2 to 3 minutes. Remove the pan from the heat and let the mixture cool to room temperature.

2. In a medium bowl, combine the butter, wine reduction, rosemary, salt, and pepper. Use a rubber spatula to stir until the mixture is smooth. Take a sheet of wax paper and place the butter on top. Shape the butter into a 2-inch-thick log, roll it in the wax paper, and twist at the ends to secure. Refrigerate the compound butter for at least 1 hour.

3. Preheat an outdoor grill to 400°F.

4. Wrap a strip of bacon around the sides of each venison medallion, and secure it to the meat with a toothpick.

5. Pat the medallions dry with a paper towel, and season both sides with salt and pepper to taste. Place the venison on the grill over direct heat and close the lid. Grill for 3 to 4 minutes per side, until the internal temperature reaches 140°F (for medium), or grill the meat to your desired degree of doneness.

6. To serve, remove the toothpicks and top each venison medallion with a slice of the compound butter. The heat from the medallion will melt the butter and create a flavorful butter sauce.

SMOKED VENISON ROAST WITH BLACKBERRY BBQ SAUCE

Roasts aren't just for slow cookers; when smoked, the meat is equally delicious. For the most tender results, brine the roast overnight; for the brine, combine 2 quarts of warm water with ½ cup kosher salt, stirring until the salt dissolves. Let it come to room temperature, then add the roast and refrigerate until you are ready to smoke. I prefer applewood chips for this recipe.

Prep Time: 15 minutes
Cook Time: 4 to 5 hours
Serves: 8 to 10

For the smoked venison roast

2 tablespoons garlic powder

1 tablespoon onion powder

1 tablespoon kosher salt

1 tablespoon packed brown sugar

2 teaspoons freshly ground black pepper

2 teaspoons dried basil

¼ teaspoon cayenne pepper

1 (3- to 4-pound) boneless venison roast

For the blackberry BBQ sauce

2 cups frozen or fresh blackberries

¾ cup apple cider vinegar

⅓ cup ketchup

1 large shallot, minced, or 2 teaspoons onion powder

2 teaspoons minced or grated fresh ginger

1 teaspoon kosher salt

½ teaspoon freshly ground black pepper

1. Preheat an electric smoker to 225°F.

2. **To prepare the smoked venison roast:** In a small bowl, combine the garlic powder, onion powder, salt, brown sugar, pepper, basil, and cayenne.

3. Pat the venison roast dry with a paper towel. Season the roast with the spice rub evenly on all sides.

4. Place the roast in the smoker. Smoke for 4 to 5 hours, until the internal temperature of 135°F (for medium), or smoke the meat to your desired degree of doneness.

5. **To make the blackberry BBQ sauce:** In a medium saucepan, combine the blackberries, vinegar, ketchup, shallot, ginger, salt, and pepper. Simmer over medium heat, stirring occasionally, for 20 minutes. Remove the pan from the heat. With an immersion blender, puree the sauce until smooth. If necessary, reheat the sauce over low heat before serving.

6. Transfer the roast to a cutting board and let it rest for 10 minutes. Slice the venison and serve it with the sauce.

Pro Tip: If you don't have an immersion blender, let the sauce cool for 10 minutes, then puree half the mixture at a time in a blender until smooth. Return the pureed sauce to the saucepan to keep warm.

SURF AND TURF VENISON KEBABS

Don't you just feel special when you have a meal of surf and turf? This recipe marries the land and sea in a garlicky butter sauce that creates quite the harmonious relationship. You will be coming back to this page in the book for years to come. Pro tip: If you're planning a camping trip, try cooking the kebabs over an open fire.

Prep Time: 15 minutes
Cook Time: 10 minutes
Serves: 4

1 cup (2 sticks) unsalted butter, melted

1 tablespoon minced garlic

1 tablespoon lemon juice

1½ teaspoons Italian seasoning

2 teaspoons kosher salt

1 teaspoon freshly ground black pepper

1 teaspoon paprika

1 pound venison tenderloin, cut into 1½-inch cubes

1 pound shrimp, peeled and deveined

1. Preheat an outdoor grill to 400°F.

2. In a large microwave-safe glass bowl, melt the butter in the microwave on high for 1 minute. Whisk in the garlic, lemon juice, Italian seasoning, salt, pepper, and paprika until combined.

3. Transfer ¼ cup of the garlic butter to a small bowl and set it aside. Add the venison and shrimp to the remaining butter in the large bowl and toss to coat well. Thread the venison and shrimp on metal skewers (or wood skewers that have been soaked in water for 30 minutes).

4. Place the skewers on the grill over direct heat, close the lid, and grill, turning every few minutes, until the meat is cooked through, about 5 to 7 minutes.

5. Transfer the kebabs to a serving platter. Brush them with the reserved garlic butter (if needed, microwave the butter for 30 seconds to remelt), then serve.

SMOKED BACKSTRAP WITH GARLICKY MUSHROOMS

6-INGREDIENT

This recipe is like going to a steak house, but you can stay in your sweatpants if you want. It's rich in flavor and pairs nicely with a glass of red wine. I keep the backstrap seasoned minimally in this recipe to let the smoke take center stage.

Prep Time: 10 minutes
Cook Time: 3 to 4 hours
Serves: 6 to 8

1 (2- to 3-pound) venison backstrap

1½ teaspoons garlic powder

Kosher salt

Freshly ground black pepper

¼ cup (½ stick) unsalted butter

1 pound white button mushrooms, sliced

6 garlic cloves, minced

1 teaspoon dried thyme

1. Set an electric smoker to 200°F.

2. Season the backstrap with the garlic powder and salt and pepper to taste.

3. Place the backstrap in the smoker. Smoke for 3 to 4 hours, until the internal temperature reaches 140°F (for medium), or smoke the meat to your desired degree of doneness.

4. About 30 minutes before the backstrap is finished cooking, prepare the mushrooms. Melt the butter in a large cast-iron pan over medium-high heat. Add the mushrooms, garlic, thyme, and salt and pepper to taste. Cook until the mushrooms are browned, 15 to 20 minutes.

5. Transfer the smoked backstrap to a cutting board and let it rest for 5 minutes. Slice the venison and serve the mushrooms on top.

SMOKED VENISON BRISKET WITH MINT CHIMICHURRI

A venison brisket is much smaller than a beef brisket, but it's just as delicious, especially when smoked and paired with the flavors of chimichurri. The coolness of the mint enhances the smoky flavor of the roast and cuts the richness, keeping you going back for more. This chimichurri is also great on beef, lamb, and wild game birds.

Prep Time: 30 minutes
Cook Time: 2 hours 30 minutes
Serves: 6 to 8

1 (3- to 4-pound) venison brisket

Kosher salt

Freshly ground black pepper

1¼ cups packed fresh mint leaves

1 cup packed fresh flat-leaf parsley leaves

1 tablespoon minced garlic

1 tablespoon lemon juice

¼ teaspoon red pepper flakes

½ cup olive oil

⅓ cup red wine vinegar

1. Preheat an electric smoker to 225°F.

2. Season the brisket generously with salt and pepper. Let the meat sit uncovered at room temperature for 30 minutes.

3. Place the brisket in the smoker. Smoke until the meat is fork-tender and its internal temperature reaches 150°F, about 2 hours.

4. While the brisket is smoking, make the chimichurri. In a food processor, combine the mint, parsley, garlic, lemon juice, red pepper flakes, olive oil, and vinegar. Pulse until the herbs are finely chopped.

5. Transfer the brisket to a cutting board and let rest for 20 minutes. To serve, slice the brisket against the grain and top the slices with the sauce.

Pro Tip: If you are used to smoking beef brisket, this 2-hour smoking time may seem like a mistake. However, because venison brisket is much smaller and lacks the collagen that beef brisket has, venison brisket can be smoked in a fraction of the time.

HAWAIIAN-INSPIRED SMOKED VENISON SHANK

6 INGREDIENT

My favorite place in the world is Hawaii. I'd be a happy camper living the beach life, snacking on tropical fruits, and smoking meats. This recipe is inspired by kalua pig, a traditional Hawaiian dish that's smoked in the ground. It has all the sweet flavors of Hawaii with just 6 ingredients, and it produces fall-off-the-bone tender meat—perfect for entertaining.

Prep Time: 10 minutes
Cook Time: 6 hours 15 minutes
Serves: 10 to 12

1 (32-ounce) bottle pineapple juice

1 cup soy sauce

½ cup honey

8 garlic cloves, minced

2 tablespoons minced or grated fresh ginger

1 (5- to 6-pound) bone-in venison shoulder

Kosher salt

Freshly ground black pepper

1. Preheat an electric smoker to 225°F.

2. In a large saucepan, combine the pineapple juice, soy sauce, honey, garlic, and ginger. Place the pan over medium-high heat and bring the mixture to a boil, stirring occasionally. Cook until the marinade has reduced by one-quarter, about 15 minutes.

3. Brush the venison shoulder with the pineapple marinade, then season the meat generously with salt and pepper. Place the shoulder in the smoker. Smoke the meat for 3 hours, basting it every 30 minutes with the pineapple marinade.

4. Place the venison shoulder in a disposable aluminum tray, and pour in the remining pineapple marinade. Raise the smoker temperature to 300°F. Smoke the venison until the meat is tender and falling off the bone and the internal temperature reaches 160°F, about another 3 hours.

CHAPTER 7

SAUSAGE AND JERKY

If you took a poll of deer hunters, I'm sure the majority would say that they mostly make sausage and jerky with their venison. In the spirit of trying to make these two preparations as easy as possible, I've come up with shortcut techniques you're going to love. For the sausage, I use the ground venison you have on hand and combine it with lard or bacon fat to make patties—no more grinding and stuffing casings. And I know you'll also enjoy my "fresh" jerky, which requires no curing salts and is ready in a fraction of the time that regular jerky takes.

VENISON BREAKFAST SAUSAGE

Sunday mornings call for venison breakfast sausage. Whether you are making pancakes or burritos, this sausage is perfect on the side. Just wait till you try these with maple syrup—hello, dreamy goodness! I like to double the recipe and freeze the extras for later uses.

Prep Time: 10 minutes
Makes: 2 pounds

2 pounds ground venison

¼ cup lard

2 teaspoons chopped
   fresh sage

1 teaspoon kosher salt

1 teaspoon freshly ground
   black pepper

½ teaspoon ground allspice

½ teaspoon garlic powder

¼ teaspoon ground nutmeg

1. In a large bowl, combine the venison, lard, sage, salt, pepper, allspice, garlic powder, and nutmeg; use your hands to mix well.

2. Form the sausage mixture into 4-ounce patties. Store the patties in an airtight container in the refrigerator for up to 6 days, or vacuum seal and freeze them for up to 3 months.

3 WAYS TO COOK VENISON SAUSAGE

All of these methods work with the sausage recipes in this chapter.

➤ GRILL IT

Preheat an outdoor grill to 375° to 400°F, setting it up for indirect cooking (see page 70). Place the patties over direct heat until browned, about 8 minutes with the lid down, then turn them over, moving them to indirect heat; close the lid and grill until cooked through, 10 to 12 minutes.

➤ COOK IT IN A SKILLET

Preheat a cast-iron skillet over medium-high heat for several minutes, add 1 tablespoon vegetable oil, tilt the skillet to coat the bottom, then add the patties. Brown on one side for 3 minutes, then turn and brown the other side until cooked through, 3 to 7 minutes.

➤ COOK IT IN THE OVEN

Preheat the oven to 350°F. Put the patties on a baking sheet. Bake until browned on one side, 5 to 7 minutes, then turn and bake until browned on the other side and cooked through, another 5 to 7 minutes.

VENISON COUNTRY SAUSAGE

Prep Time: 10 minutes
Makes: 2 pounds

2 pounds ground venison

¼ pound bacon, chopped into small pieces

¼ cup dry white wine

1 tablespoon paprika

1½ teaspoons dried sage

1 teaspoon kosher salt

½ teaspoon freshly ground black pepper

1. In a large bowl, combine the venison, bacon, wine, paprika, sage, salt, and pepper; use your hands to mix well.

2. Form the sausage meat into 4-ounce patties. Store the patties in an airtight container in the refrigerator for up to 6 days, or vacuum seal and freeze them for up to 3 months.

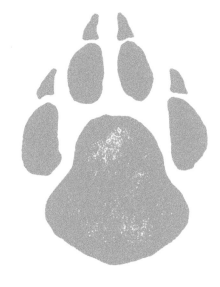

VENISON AND MUSHROOM SAUSAGE

This recipe is inspired by fall, full of earthy, herby flavor. Enjoy it cooked up with breakfast, or use it to stuff a venison (or pork) loin or Thanksgiving turkey.

Prep Time: 15 minutes, plus
2 hours to chill
Makes: 1½ pounds

1 pound ground venison

¼ cup lard

1 large onion, diced

½ cup minced mushrooms,
   such as cremini, portobello,
   or porcini

3 tablespoons minced garlic

2 teaspoons kosher salt

1 teaspoon freshly ground
   black pepper

1 teaspoon dried sage

1 teaspoon dried basil

1. In a large bowl, combine the venison, lard, onion, mushrooms, garlic, salt, pepper, sage, and basil; use your hands to mix well. Cover and refrigerate for 2 hours.

2. Form the sausage meat into 4-ounce patties. Store the patties in an airtight container in the refrigerator for up to 6 days, or vacuum seal and freeze them for up to 3 months.

CHORIZO-STYLE VENISON SAUSAGE

I basically grew up on chorizo-and-egg and chorizo-and-potato burritos. If you want to make a dish better, just throw some chorizo in it. This Spanish-style sausage is packed with flavor, and it's delicious cooked up on its own or used as an ingredient in other recipes.

Prep Time: 15 minutes
Makes: 2 pounds

2 pounds ground venison

½ cup distilled white vinegar

¼ cup chili powder

3 tablespoons paprika

2 tablespoons rendered
  bacon fat

2 tablespoons minced garlic

1½ tablespoons ground cumin

2 teaspoons kosher salt

2 teaspoons dried oregano

1½ teaspoons ground cinnamon

¼ teaspoon ground cloves

1. In a large bowl, combine the venison, vinegar, chili powder, paprika, bacon fat, garlic, cumin, salt, oregano, cinnamon, and cloves; use your hands to mix well.

2. Form the sausage meat into 4-ounce patties. Store the patties in an airtight container in the refrigerator for up to 6 days, or vacuum seal and freeze them for up to 3 months.

CLASSIC BBQ GROUND VENISON JERKY

6-INGREDIENT

This jerky has a hint of both smoke and heat, and you can change it up by using different kinds of barbecue sauce. To make jerky with ground meat, you've got to invest in a jerky gun and a dehydrator. They're not expensive, and you'll be glad you made the investments.

Prep Time: 15 minutes, plus 24 hours to marinate
Cook Time: 3 hours
Makes: 40 to 50 pieces

2 pounds ground venison

¼ cup barbecue sauce

1 tablespoon liquid smoke

2 teaspoons Worcestershire sauce

½ teaspoon cayenne pepper

1. In a large bowl, combine the venison, barbecue sauce, liquid smoke, Worcestershire sauce, and cayenne; use your hands to mix well.

2. Place the meat mixture in a jerky gun, making sure to pack it tight to avoid any air pockets. Close the jerky gun and dispense 5- to 6-inch strips onto dehydrator trays, leaving about 1 inch between each strip. Make sure you have a paring knife handy so you can cut each strip off from the jerky gun.

3. Set a dehydrator to 160°F.

4. Dehydrate the meat mixture for 3 hours, then check the jerky. When it is done, it should be pliable and able to bend without breaking. If it feels moist, continue to dehydrate; depending on the level of humidity, this can take up to 6 hours. Check for doneness every hour.

5. Remove the jerky from the dehydrator and let it cool to room temperature. Store in an airtight container at room temperature for up to 4 weeks or in the refrigerator for up to 5 weeks.

JERKY TIPS

Jerky is one of the best ways to preserve your harvest. To make these recipes super simple, I did not include curing salts, and I cut back on the dehydrating time. Normally jerky takes 10 to 12 hours to properly dehydrate, but the dehydration time for these recipes is about 3 hours. The result is what I like to call "fresh jerky." Just be aware that it has a shorter shelf life than regular jerky, around 4 weeks at room temperature and 5 weeks if you refrigerate it.

Here are a few tips to ensure jerky success.

➤ If you're using whole pieces of meat, freeze them for 30 to 45 minutes before cutting. This will make it easier to slice thin pieces.

➤ If you have a slicer, use it to ensure that all the slices are the same thickness.

➤ Buy silica gel packets to place inside the airtight container your jerky is stored in; this will help keep out moisture, which causes jerky to spoil.

➤ To check for doneness, remove a jerky piece from the dehydrator, let it cool for about 5 minutes, and then bend it in half; it should be flexible enough that it won't break, and there should be no liquid present.

BOURBON-BROWN SUGAR VENISON JERKY

6-INGREDIENT

Bourbon is not only a fantastic libation on its own, it is also absolutely stunning when paired with venison. This recipe is a favorite because the bourbon gets dehydrated and all those rich, intense flavors are infused into the jerky. Use a good bourbon—don't go cheap here—because you will taste the difference.

Prep Time: 15 minutes, plus overnight to marinate
Cook Time: 3 hours
Makes: 20 to 30 pieces

¼ cup bourbon

2 tablespoons packed dark brown sugar

1 tablespoon kosher salt or sea salt

1 teaspoon freshly ground black pepper

Grated zest of 1 orange

2 pounds venison meat, such as bottom round, sliced against the grain ⅛- to ¼-inch thick

1. In a large bowl, whisk together the bourbon, sugar, salt, pepper, and orange zest until the sugar and salt have completely dissolved. Add the venison strips and toss to coat well. Cover and refrigerate overnight.

2. Set the dehydrator to 145°F.

3. Gently shake off any excess marinade from the venison, and place the venison strips on dehydrator trays so they do not touch. Dehydrate for 3 hours or until the jerky is pliable.

4. Remove the jerky from the dehydrator and let cool to room temperature. Store in an airtight container at room temperature for up to 4 weeks or in the refrigerator for up to 5 weeks.

BLOODY MARY VENISON JERKY

If you're a brunch enthusiast like me, you can appreciate a good Bloody Mary. The salty, savory, pickled, and spicy flavors are utterly delicious. I took this favorite cocktail and turned it into jerky, and the result is pure joy. If you are feeling adventurous, switch out the horseradish for 2 teaspoons of wasabi paste.

Prep Time: 15 minutes, plus overnight to marinate
Cook Time: 3 to 4 hours
Makes: 20 to 30 pieces

1 cup Bloody Mary mix

¼ cup Worcestershire sauce

¼ cup soy sauce

1 tablespoon dill pickle juice

1½ teaspoons celery salt

1½ teaspoons prepared horseradish

1 teaspoon Old Bay seasoning

2 pounds venison meat, such as bottom round, sliced against the grain ⅛- to ¼-inch thick

1. In a large bowl, whisk together the Bloody Mary mix, Worcestershire sauce, soy sauce, pickle juice, celery salt, horseradish, and Old Bay. Add the venison strips and toss to coat well. Cover and refrigerate overnight.

2. Set the dehydrator to 150°F.

3. Gently shake off any excess marinade, and place the venison strips on dehydrator trays so they do not touch. Dehydrate for 3 to 4 hours or until the jerky is pliable.

4. Remove the jerky from the dehydrator and let cool to room temperature. Store in an airtight container at room temperature for up to 4 weeks or in the refrigerator for up to 5 weeks.

CITRUS-BASIL VENISON JERKY

Citrus and venison make a great pairing. The acid in the citrus helps to break down and tenderize the meat while imparting a great sour-sweet flavor. This recipe was inspired by a citrus and basil sauce I ate in Capri, Italy.

Prep Time: 15 minutes, plus 3 hours to marinate
Cook Time: 3 to 4 hours
Makes: 20 to 30 pieces

½ cup orange juice

¼ cup soy sauce

2 tablespoons dried basil

1 tablespoon grated orange zest

1 tablespoon grated lemon zest

1 tablespoon grated lime zest

1 teaspoon garlic powder

¼ teaspoon cayenne pepper (optional)

2 pounds venison meat, such as bottom round, sliced against the grain ⅛- to ¼-inch thick

1. In a large bowl, whisk together the orange juice, soy sauce, basil, orange zest, lemon zest, lime zest, garlic powder, and cayenne (if using). Add the venison strips and toss to coat well. Cover and refrigerate for 3 hours.

2. Set the dehydrator to 145°F.

3. Gently shake off any excess marinade, and place the venison strips on the dehydrator trays so they do not touch. Dehydrate for 3 to 4 hours or until the jerky is pliable.

4. Remove the jerky from the dehydrator and let cool to room temperature. Store in an airtight container at room temperature for up to 4 weeks or in the refrigerator for up to 5 weeks.

PINEAPPLE-JALAPEÑO-LIME VENISON JERKY

6-INGREDIENT

If you're a fan of sweet and spicy—a common Hawaiian pairing—this recipe is for you. When I was road-tripping in Hawaii, I grabbed a bag of Maui Gold pineapple and jalapeño-flavored bison jerky, and it was probably the best jerky I have ever had. This is my ode to that amazing bag of jerky that I will never forget.

Prep Time: 15 minutes, plus overnight to marinate
Cook Time: 3 hours
Makes: 20 to 30 pieces

½ cup pineapple juice

3 tablespoons soy sauce

3 tablespoons honey

1 tablespoon grated lime zest

2 teaspoons minced jalapeño

2 pounds venison meat, such as bottom round, sliced against the grain ⅛- to ¼-inch thick

1. In a large bowl, whisk together the pineapple juice, soy sauce, honey, lime zest, and jalapeño. Add the venison strips and toss to coat well. Cover and refrigerate overnight.

2. Set the dehydrator to 145°F.

3. Gently shake off any excess marinade, and place the venison strips on dehydrator trays so they do not touch. Dehydrate for 3 hours or until the jerky is pliable.

4. Remove the jerky from the dehydrator and let to cool to room temperature. Store in an airtight container at room temperature for up to 4 weeks or in the refrigerator for up to 5 weeks.

FIVE-SPICE VENISON JERKY WITH SESAME SEEDS

If you love the flavors of teriyaki, you will flip for this. The sesame seeds are key; I sprinkle them on the jerky before it goes into the dehydrator so they stick. They add a crunch factor that really elevates the jerky.

Prep Time: 15 minutes, plus 5 hours to marinate
Cook Time: 3 hours
Makes: 20 to 30 strips

½ cup soy sauce

½ cup fish sauce

1 tablespoon balsamic vinegar

1 tablespoon packed brown sugar

2 teaspoons five-spice powder

1 teaspoon garlic powder

2 pounds venison meat, such as bottom round, sliced against the grain ⅛- to ¼-inch thick

¼ cup sesame seeds

1. In a large bowl, whisk together the soy sauce, fish sauce, vinegar, brown sugar, five-spice powder, and garlic powder. Add the venison strips and toss to coat well. Cover and refrigerate for at least 5 hours or overnight.

2. Set the dehydrator to 145°F.

3. Gently shake off any excess marinade, and place the strips on dehydrator trays so they do not touch. Sprinkle the sesame seeds evenly over the strips. Dehydrate for 3 hours or until the jerky is pliable.

4. Remove the jerky from the dehydrator and let cool to room temperature. Store in an airtight container at room temperature for up to 4 weeks or in the refrigerator for up to 5 weeks.

MEASUREMENT CONVERSIONS

VOLUME EQUIVALENTS (LIQUID)

US STANDARD	US STANDARD (OUNCES)	METRIC (APPROX.)
2 tablespoons	1 fl. oz.	30 mL
¼ cup	2 fl. oz.	60 mL
½ cup	4 fl. oz.	120 mL
1 cup	8 fl. oz.	240 mL
1½ cups	12 fl. oz.	355 mL
2 cups or 1 pint	16 fl. oz.	475 mL
4 cups or 1 quart	32 fl. oz.	1 L
1 gallon	128 fl. oz.	4 L

OVEN TEMPERATURES

FAHRENHEIT (F)	CELSIUS (C) (APPROX.)
250°	120°
300°	150°
325°	165°
350°	180°
375°	190°
400°	200°
425°	220°
450°	230°

VOLUME EQUIVALENTS (DRY)

US STANDARD	METRIC (APPROX.)
⅛ teaspoon	0.5 mL
¼ teaspoon	1 mL
½ teaspoon	2 mL
¾ teaspoon	4 mL
1 teaspoon	5 mL
1 tablespoon	15 mL
¼ cup	59 mL
⅓ cup	79 mL
½ cup	118 mL
⅔ cup	156 mL
¾ cup	177 mL
1 cup	235 mL
2 cups or 1 pint	475 mL
3 cups	700 mL
4 cups or 1 quart	1 L

WEIGHT EQUIVALENTS

US STANDARD	METRIC (APPROX.)
½ ounce	15 g
1 ounce	30 g
2 ounces	60 g
4 ounces	115 g
8 ounces	225 g
12 ounces	340 g
16 ounces or 1 pound	455 g

INDEX

ACKNOWLEDGMENTS

I'd like to give a big thank-you to my publisher, Callisto Media, for letting me show people the beautiful world of wild game!

A big thank you to Pam Kingsley, who has championed my books and worked so hard on this one. And thank you to Anne Egan, who has so kindly worked with me to turn my chef brain recipes into recipes that everyone can make.

Thank you to all my followers who inspired a lot of these recipes; this book is truly for you!

ABOUT THE AUTHOR

Born and raised in sunny California, **BRI VAN SCOTTER** grew up riding horses and racing dirt bikes. She also didn't grow up hunting. When it was time to head to college, Bri's first choice was culinary school, but she understood the value of a university degree. So, she went on to graduate from California State University Fullerton. After graduation, her degree landed her a job at a large retailer; however, that job meant she would sit in a cubicle all day. Not keen on that kind of life, Bri got a job as a hostess in the evenings at a local restaurant. Having a huge passion for cooking and baking, Bri quickly ended up in the pastry department and was thrown on the line rather quickly. Baking desserts at the restaurant became something she looked forward to every day. It was then that she decided to head to culinary school to pursue her passion, graduating from the Culinary Institute of America in Napa, California, with a degree in Culinary Arts and then an additional degree from the Art Institute of Orange County, California.

With two culinary degrees, Bri has worked in some of the most prestigious restaurants in the United States. She has worked as both an executive chef and executive pastry chef. But, it wasn't until a move to Georgia that she discovered her love for hunting. Her husband bought her a bow, which he thought would be just for fun, and ended up changing her career. Six months later, she was in a tree stand on opening day getting her first doe. After her first harvest, she had an abundance of wild protein but noticed there was a lack of wild game recipes. So, she created Wilderness to Table, a website dedicated to self-harvested wild game recipes.

Her blog started to gain momentum, and soon she was writing wild game recipes and articles for magazines, one of which caught the eye of a producer, and her blog was turned into a television show that is now available on Amazon Prime and iTunes. Bri has appeared on news segments, gives cooking demonstrations all over the United States, and is an advocate for hunting and conservation. Bri now travels the world to hunt. She is an avid upland bird shooter and can always be seen with her bird dog by her side.

To learn more about Bri, head to her website, WildernesstoTable.com, or visit her on Instagram @WildernessToTable. There, she shares more wild game recipes and offers a glimpse into her world as an avid hunter, scuba diver, spear fisher, free diver, and traveler.

Printed in the USA
CPSIA information can be obtained
at www.ICGtesting.com
LVHW061321171223
766457LV00002B/26

9 781647 398101